Published by Grayson Consulting LLC.

978-0-9854411-5-9
August 2017
Version 1.1

Table of Contents

Preface

As an undergraduate, I completed a double major in biology and literature. After college, I conducted research in a lab. These formative experiences influence how I approach problems.

When I moved into the business world, my first job included managing email campaigns. Once I'd created and mastered the process for sending the campaigns, I got a little bored. So I started playing a game: How much could I improve the results? I introduced changes, tracked user behavior and rolled successful changes over into the next set of emails. I couldn't split test but by making iterative changes, I got great results. User engagement doubled and the number of email campaigns sold increased dramatically.

From optimizing emails it was an easy step to optimizing websites. I started site testing as a hackathon project. A key page on the marketing site needed improvement. Not content to just make changes, I ran an A/B test to measure the impact of the new page. The results were impressive and I was hooked on website optimization.

I have successfully optimized many websites. I created the Six Steps process based on what drives results.

I hope you find the Six Steps useful and that this book will lead you to a more successful site.

Tabitha Grayson
August 2017
books@grysn.com

Introduction

This is a book about how to create an exceptional website specific to your company and your audience. I won't be offering one-size-fits-all website changes, but I will show you the steps to create a successful site.

How this book will help you

A successful site needs an audience motivated to perform actions the company views as valuable. To discover how to motivate your audience, you have to understand them.

In this book, I will introduce you to the Six Steps, an evidence-based process for optimizing websites. You'll start with a clear view of what your company needs and develop insight into your audience through testing and research. The more you know about your audience, the stronger you can make your site.

People new to improving websites will find a process for discovering and implementing effective site changes. Old hands will find an evidence-based approach that takes familiar ideas and threads them together into a coherent solution that is stronger than its parts.

Search for knowledge

The Six Steps is a modified version of the scientific method.

The scientific method is an essential tool of modern science. Scientists use the scientific method to make discoveries based on evidence rather than relying on biases and opinions.

When you follow the Six Steps, you'll start by studying the site, the audience and the company goals. As with the scientific method, you'll follow the evidence. This will take your ideas in new and unexpected directions. The more knowledge you have the better your ideas, and, when you act on your best ideas, you get the best results.

The Six Steps, like the scientific method, is a repetitive cycle. You build on prior knowledge to develop a deeper and richer understanding of how to create an exceptional site.

The Six Steps

The Six Steps is a modified version of the scientific method. While the scientific method works best in reproducible environments, the Six Steps works in constantly shifting environments like websites.

The scientific method, modified

The scientific method is a powerful tool that scientists use to make new discoveries and breakthroughs. The intent of the scientific method is to discover what's real and what can be proven, instead of relying on biases and preformed opinions.

No theory or idea in science is absolute – new information can prove an idea wrong. Paradoxically, this openness to being wrong makes the scientific method a powerful tool for discovering what's true. When all ideas can be challenged, no wrong idea can permanently hinder the search for knowledge.

The Six Steps incorporates principles of the scientific method but is designed for optimizing websites.

During the observation and question stages of the Six Steps, you'll draw in as much information as you can and throw as wide a net as possible. In later steps, you'll focus on what to change on the site and why those changes will work.

The Six Steps, like the scientific method, is a repetitive cycle. You'll add observations, questions and test results over time. During this process you'll gain a richer and deeper understanding of the audience. This body of knowledge will help you predict audience behavior and find new opportunities and strategies.

Step 1: Define the problem

The first step is to define the problem. With a clearly defined problem, you will know what you need to address and can focus your resources effectively.

In this step, examine the company's mission, goals and challenges, and talk to stakeholders. Then create a site objective that states the problem you want to solve and your goals. Once you have a final draft of the site objective, you'll need to get sign off from the decisions makers. The decision makers vary depending on the company but they often include executives.

To illustrate the steps, in this chapter we'll be following a fictional character, Henry.

> Henry has been assigned to improve the website's performance. Since this is vague (it could refer to time for the pages to load, revenue, traffic, branding, etc.) he does some digging. Henry speaks with stakeholders, and researches company goals and challenges to learn what's needed. After several rounds of discussions and research, he develops and receives approval on the site objective: "Increase site revenue by 10% over the next 3 months".

Step 2: Observations

Once you've defined your site objective, the next step is to make observations. You'll use existing information and might conduct additional research.

As you gather information, look for patterns. Note where information is consistent, where it is inconsistent, and consider why that might be the case.

Make sure you keep track of your observations in a readily accessible place. This is a repetitive cycle. You will add more observations to your list as you move through the Six Steps.

> Henry learns that the company focuses on making a large number of low value sales. Individually the low value sales are not very profitable but combined they produce significant revenue. As a result, the site's design has mostly focused on encouraging the sale of inexpensive products as have the acquisition marketing campaigns.

Step 3: Questions

In the previous step you gathered observations and began thinking about how the information could be connected.

During this step, think of questions based on your observations. Note all questions whether they are small or big.

You'll create many questions. As with observations, you should record these and keep them to refer to later. You'll also add to your list of questions as you follow the Six Steps.

Don't get too invested in one idea at this stage. There's more work to do before an idea is proved or disproved.

> Henry does some digging and uncovers a graph of the purchase distribution. The graph shows the number of orders for each order size:

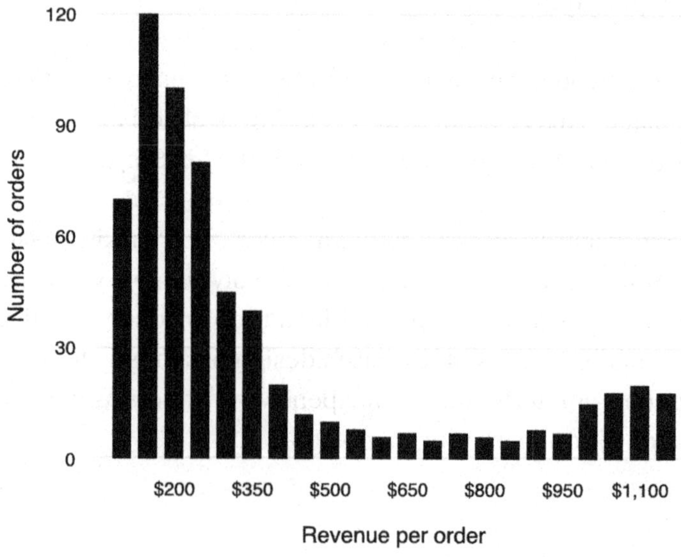

For example, there are 70 orders with a revenue per order of $50.

By looking at the graph, Henry can see that most of the orders are low value.

He formulates the question: 'How would this graph look if I analyzed revenue instead?'.

Henry calculates the revenue associated with each point on the graph using this equation:

(Number of Orders) × (Revenue Per Order) = Revenue

For instance, there are 20 orders with a revenue per order of $1,100. Henry uses the equation to calculate the revenue:

(20 orders) × ($1,100/order) = $22,000

Once Henry has calculated the revenue for each set of orders, he builds a new graph:

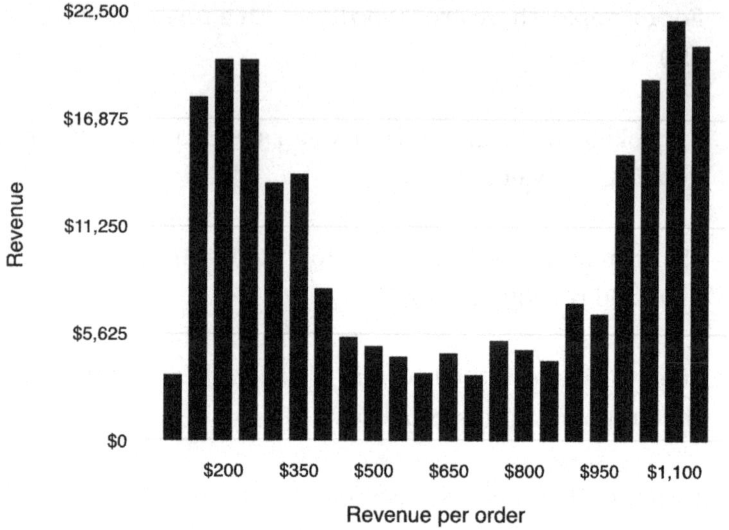

When Henry looks at this new graph he can see two revenue peaks, one at either end of the revenue per order axis.

The low value orders are an important source of revenue, but so are the high value orders. By ignoring the high value orders, the company is overlooking a profitable segment.

Step 4: Hypotheses

A hypothesis is a statement that explains the observable facts. You can prove the explanation right or wrong by testing it.

You can also think of a hypothesis as a testable user story. You predict users will behave in a certain way and then you can test to see if you're right.

Henry knows from his earlier work that there are two peaks

of revenue. The first peak of revenue comes from the buyers who make low value orders. The second peak comes from buyers who make high value orders.

He hypothesizes that individuals make the low value orders and that companies make the high value orders. In other words, a lot of individuals make inexpensive purchases and a few companies make expensive purchases.

Step 5: Testing

In a lab, it's straightforward for scientists to set up and test a hypothesis. Scientists run tests in a controlled environment so no unexpected variables upset the results. For instance, scientists sometimes run tests on yeast. Every yeast is genetically identical and kept in the exact same conditions. The only change is the variable the scientist introduces.

This approach won't work on a website. There are many variables that can impact your results. A/B testing helps address this, but doesn't necessarily solve it. (I'll go over A/B testing in more detail in a later chapter.) However, you can still develop significant insights by pursuing answers with a methodical and rational approach.

When testing a hypothesis, you must be open to being wrong, and adjust course accordingly. If you can't face being wrong, this process will fail because you will believe your results are correct when they are just your opinion.

Henry asks the data analyst to examine the distribution of

company names associated with purchases and how it matches up against the revenue graph.

His hypothesis is that companies are making most of the high value orders. If this hypothesis is true, it follows that a high percentage of the high value orders will have a company name associated with them.

The analyst looks at the data. 80% of the high value orders have a company name associated with the purchase. The low value orders have a company name associated with them 5% of the time. This suggests companies make the high value orders and individuals make the low value orders. However, as the checkout process does not require customers to enter a company name, more research is needed.

Step 6: The big picture

In science, a theory is a conclusion that explains phenomena and predicts behavior. It is supported by proven hypotheses. It is hard to create theories for a website. Variables beyond your control make it difficult to create statements that are always true.

You can find evidence, though, that provides insight into your audience and the motivations for their behavior. Once you have gathered enough information you can create a big picture idea of your audience. The big picture will help you predict how your audience will react to site changes. When you take the big picture into account your site changes will be more successful. When you run more successful tests, you'll optimize your site faster.

Henry pursues his hypothesis that businesses make most of the high value orders and individuals make most of the low value orders. He collects observations, asks questions, constructs hypotheses and runs tests. Henry builds a case that sales to the previously unidentified audience group, businesses, are critical.

Henry produces a new site section for businesses. The overall company revenue increases by 15%. The increase in revenue comes from high value business orders.

Henry continues to add to his observations, create new questions and test hypotheses. His understanding of audience motivations and goals becomes more nuanced. As he gains more knowledge, he makes smarter decisions, runs better tests and optimizes the site faster.

Challenges and advantages

The Six Steps has many of the strengths of the scientific method, but is adapted for website work.

Challenges

Sites are altered frequently, the audience shifts regularly, and business needs may change. Date is often not entirely reliable, which adds uncertainty to your conclusions. You won't publish your results in a peer-reviewed journal and results may only be reproducible on one site.

These challenges make it difficult to optimize a website with the scientific method. The Six Steps, though, is more flexible and designed to work within these limitations.

Advantages

The Six Steps method champions rational, data-driven results over opinions, biases and fashions.

With the information you learn about your audience, you can develop stronger site strategies. By following data you can find what other people never thought to look for and make breakthroughs for your site.

A key advantage of the Six Steps is that you can be wrong. When you admit that you could be wrong, it is easier to see errors and take in new information. People who hold onto being right don't learn. They get stuck in a quagmire of their own opinions and can't figure out why what they're doing isn't working.

Finally, if you can back up your proposals with facts, it is much easier to persuade other people that you have good ideas, and to get buy in and support.

The upshot

People often use parts of the scientific method without even thinking about it – they draw information from multiple sources, develop ideas about what's going on, and then make changes based on those ideas.

However, most people are not consistent in this approach or self-critical enough. They are blind to errors because they become passionately attached to an idea.

The Six Steps helps you avoid these problems. It will give you insight into what to test, what to change, and how to win.

Order

In this chapter, I've described the Six Steps as if it follows a straight path from defining your site objective through to the big picture. In reality it's more fluid. Your site objective will probably stay the same unless there is a significant business change. But you will add new observations and questions constantly. For instance, a test might fail to support a hypothesis but create new observations that drive new questions and eventually a whole new hypothesis. So don't worry if you move backward; just be careful not to move forward unless you have enough information to do so.

Chapter summary

- The scientific method is a process that scientists follow to help them make new discoveries.
- The goal of the scientific method is to explain phenomenon rationally, not to prop up opinions and biases. A key

part of the scientific method is openness to being wrong.

- The Six Steps are based on the scientific method, modified for the realities of website work.

- In the observation and question steps, you gather a lot of information. You become steadily more focused in later steps as you develop a clearer understanding of your audience. The Six Steps are:

  - Step 1: Define the problem
  - Step 2: Observations
  - Step 3: Questions
  - Step 4: Hypotheses
  - Step 5: Testing
  - Step 6: The big picture

- While you can follow the Six Steps chronologically, in practice you're likely to jump around. This is fine if you only move forward when you have enough information to do so.

Step 1: Define the Problem

Just as a scientist needs to decide what area she is going to research, you need to discover what problem you are going to solve. Depending on your circumstances, this may be handed to you, you may need to refine existing ideas, or you may need to identify the problem on your own.

Having a clear idea of the problem you are solving will direct and give shape to your observations, questions, and hypotheses. A clearly defined problem makes it easier to wade through information. You can tell if information is relevant, not relevant but worth noting for a future day, or can be shelved. Without a clearly defined problem, everything is interesting and nothing takes priority.

Further down the road, a clearly defined problem and goal make it much easier to prioritize features and defend your project.

Figure out the problem you're solving as soon as you can and get buy in from decision makers. If you don't get this right and don't find the problem you need to solve, your work is unlikely to be viewed as successful.

Identifying the right problem

To identify the right problem, start by examining the company's mission, goals and challenges. Think about how your work will need to take these into account.

Talk to stakeholders. Learn what goals the stakeholders need to meet and what their pain points are. Pay particular attention to what stakeholders need versus what they say they want. Keep in mind that each stakeholder is likely to have a slightly different idea about what you are doing and why.

Compose a concise formal statement that outlines your goals and what problem you will solve. This is your site objective.

In most cases, you should include the metrics you will judge success by. If you are optimizing a site for eCommerce conversions, your metric will typically be revenue. However, you may need to optimize for a different type of metric. For instance, if you're improving a support site, revenue wouldn't make sense as the metric.

No matter what type of site you are working on, constructing a site objective is necessary. Companies can be unfocused about the purpose of their site. (I've found this to be the case even for eCommerce sites.) A site objective ensures everyone is on the same page.

Circulate the site objective for review to stakeholders and decision makers. Make sure you tie it back into the bigger company picture so people understand why they should support the project. The greater buy in you can get for your site objective, the easier it will be to move your projects forward.

During this process, be open to feedback. It can be very useful. Feedback will help you identify errors in your logic and understand the positions of stakeholders better.

Don't be afraid, though, to push back if what people are saying doesn't fit with what you've learned about company goals and challenges.

Sometimes a stakeholder has the right idea but the wrong metric (see the Indicators section below for more information). When this happens, make sure you understand the stakeholder's goals. If your site objective lines up with what the stakeholder needs, it's straightforward to draw a connection between your site objective and their metrics.

You and the stakeholders may have different ideas about what problem you need to solve. It's good to find that out early so it can be addressed before a lot of work is done. It may mean you got off on the wrong track, company goals are unclear or, more commonly, two different groups are trying to solve two different problems with one project.

Once you have the misunderstandings and misdirections sorted out, you can finalize your site objective. Make sure you get buy in from the decision makers, e.g. upper management.

Understand your metrics

Metrics only make sense when you look at the whole picture.

For example, you may see false negatives. A false negative is when it looks like a change has failed even though it is working. There are a few ways this can happen. A common cause is a change in the competitive landscape. Perhaps you improve your site but a competitor releases a better product the audience likes more. The audience buys the competitor's product and your site revenue decreases. This is a false negative because it looks like the site changes failed, even though they were successful. The decrease in revenue is because the competitive landscape changed, not because the site changes failed.

On the flip side are false positives. A false positive is when it looks like a change is working but it hasn't made any difference. Suppose you are optimizing a support site to increase the number of visits. While you're optimizing the site, marketing campaigns increase the number of customers. The changes to the support site had no positive impact, but since more people use the product more people visit the support site. In this case it would be a false positive. It would look like the changes had worked even though they didn't make a difference.

Numbers by themselves make little sense. You need to interpret them in the context of their environment.

Indicators

You can do exactly what you've been asked to do and still end up with poor results.

An example of how this can happen:

A company hires Beatrice to grow their website's audience. She makes many changes including adding a new blog, running an aggressive social media strategy and sending out regular press releases. She adds value to the company and the audience numbers increase. But her work isn't seen as successful because there is no increase in revenue. The executives never said so, but they assumed that more traffic would mean more revenue. Beatrice does exactly what the company asked her to do, and she does it well, but her work is seen as a failure because she doesn't deliver what the company needs.

You will run into difficulties when people focus on indicators (in this case, increase audience size) rather than on the problem that needs to be solved (increase revenue). An indicator is a metric influenced by the metric you should solve for. However, there is not a one-to-one correlation between the metric you should solve for and the indicator.

This sounds self-evident, but it is a common problem. People often confuse what they should track with a secondary data point.

When you build your site objective, and talk to stakeholders, keep indicators in mind. You may be asked to improve indicators. Indicators, though, are not what you need to improve. If you build your goals around the correct metrics, your site is much more likely to be successful.

Other considerations

In an ideal world, the site objective would never alter and the only site changes you'd need to make are the ones that forward your goals. The real world isn't like that, though.

Occasionally it is necessary to rewrite the site objective because business requirements change. An advantage of a clearly defined site objective is that it forces a re-assessment of the project. When a site objective is rewritten, it helps clarify how the project should change. Without a formal rewriting there's a tendency to tinker rather than to rethink the goals of the project and if they still apply. The project ends up being neither one thing nor the other, and no one's satisfied with the outcome.

Multiple stakeholders have an interest in the website. While the site objective should be your main focus, you may need to make site changes that do not support your goals.

For instance, even if your goal is to increase revenue, you might be responsible for improving the job listings on the site. While this doesn't impact revenue, it makes it easier to hire new people, which is important for long-term success. A clear site objective is helpful because it is easier to communicate trade-offs to management. You might need to tell executives that updating the job listings would delay work on improving revenue by six weeks. This prevents management from expecting you to work on all projects at the same time and keeps you focused on what to get back to once the secondary project is complete.

Chapter summary

- Create a clear site objective to focus your work on key goals. A site objective includes the problem you are solving and your goals.

- A clear site objective helps you know what ideas to pursue and what to put to one side as interesting but irrelevant.

- To find out what problem you need to solve, study company goals and challenges, and talk to stakeholders. Compose a succinct site objective and get sign off from the decision makers.

- An indicator is a metric influenced by the metric you want to improve, but isn't that metric and isn't a one-to-one correlation with that metric. For instance, an increase in audience numbers may result in an increase in revenue, but the two are not a one-to-one correlation.

- Watch out for indicators. You may be asked to create goals for them, but they're not what you need to improve.

- A website is many things to many people. You may need to do work that doesn't address the goals in your site objective. This is fine and expected. Communicate, though, how the new projects will impact the goals you are seeking to meet.

- You will need to rewrite your site objective when business requirements change. By rewriting the site objective, you create a clearly defined change. Without a new site objective, you're likely to try to apply the old site objective to the new situation which gives poor results.

Ideas are easier to remember through stories. To help us out, we'll be following Susan's work at a fictional business called the Fancy Cake Company.

Define the problem

Susan is a new hire at the Fancy Cake Company, a rapidly growing start up in the San Francisco Bay Area. They have offices downtown and all the desserts you can eat.

The Fancy Cake Company is the Etsy of baked goods. Artisan bakeries post pictures, information and prices and sell through the Fancy Cake Company site. Each product is displayed on a unique product page. Individual bakeries have a "store" which includes all their product pages.

The bakeries gain a much bigger audience by selling through the Fancy Cake Company and customers find unique artisan cakes from all over the United States.

The Fancy Cake Company hired Susan because the company is struggling with how to improve their website. Susan will direct changes to the site.

Susan's first step is to understand the company goals and what exactly "improve" means.

The company has had steady growth over the past 12 months, but wants to rapidly expand over the next two years. Currently the Fancy Cake Company is the only company of this type in the market, but the founders expect other venture capital-funded groups to put sites live soon.

Susan speaks with many stakeholders about the site. They have different opinions on how she should improve the site.

The director of design argues for a new color scheme, the marketing manager in charge of branding wants to add a blog, and the head of sales pushes for more business promotions.

After working with key stakeholders, and researching company strategy, Susan identifies that the core goal is to increase revenue. The stakeholders have good ideas, but they focus on *how* Susan should solve the problem rather than on what needs solving.

Susan creates this site objective:

"Increase revenue generated by the Fancy Cake Company website by 50% over the next 12 months."

While she consulted with multiple stakeholders, Susan only needs approval on the site objective from the VP of Marketing and the CEO. They sign off on the site objective and Susan shares the final version with the team.

Step 2: Observations

Once you have finalized your site objective, your next step is to make and collect observations. Use your observations as the basis for smarter, evidence-based decisions. When you base your decisions on evidence, you'll be more likely to meet your goals.

In this section we'll explore where to find information and discuss audience motivations and state of mind.

By pulling together your observations, you'll lay the groundwork for creating questions.

Research

There is often a surprising amount of information available. To get started, I've listed a handful of places to collect observations and included some of their strengths and weaknesses.

Web analytics

Typically, when people think of data they think of site data. Examples of site data include the number of visits, most popular pages, and bounce rates.

Google Analytics is a popular service for tracking user behavior, but there are many alternatives. People often supplement their main web reporting with services that specialize in tracking a specific type of user behavior. For example, they might use a service that tracks where users move their cursor.

Site data is very useful. It is extremely difficult to optimize a site without reliable web analytics reports.

When interpreting site data, there are two basic approaches. The first is answering specific questions. A common example is recording the number of site visits for a monthly dashboard. The second is searching for information to gain insight into audience behavior. For example, digging into what users do directly before and after they trigger an event on a product page.

You might find it helpful to think of site data as an abstract representation of user behavior. Rather than thinking of data as numbers, think of it as patterns that reveal what your users are doing on the site. For instance, which pages do users visit most? Why do they visit some pages more than others? What does this tell you about user goals? In this case, you compare data to help you understand your users and what's motivating them.

The biggest strength of web analytics is that the reports contain valuable information about user behavior. If the tracking code is implemented correctly and the data is pulled properly, site data is reliable and very useful.

A major weakness for many people is that they are uncomfortable analyzing numbers. One way around this discomfort is to think of data as revealing patterns rather than as a column of numbers to crunch.

A second weakness is that reports can be inaccurate. Inaccuracies have their root in how the site analytics code works, with how the code is implemented, and with human errors in interpreting the data.

For instance, your analytics system probably tracks users by setting cookies on their browsers. If a user habitually uses two different browsers that user can show up as a new user twice. The same overcounting issue holds true if they clear their cookies.

Errors in code implementation also create reporting errors. For instance, if your developer forgets to add the tracking code to a new page, then everyone who visits that page looks like they're leaving the site. This causes metrics such as bounce rates, time on site, and number of visits to be incorrect.

I've also seen misunderstandings of how the analytics system works and the terminology it employs. These misunderstandings can result in minor data issues all the way to whole sets of data being badly corrupted and unusable.

Human errors of interpretation can introduce confusion. Suppose a company has a SaaS product that users log in to. Users reach the log in page from the homepage. When calculating visits to the site, does that include the people who are there to log in? or just prospects? It depends on how the question "How many visits are there to the site?" is meant and interpreted.

As long as either you or the analyst is diligent, your reports will be directionally correct and you can use them as a baseline for your analysis. Even though web data is not perfect, it can be reliable and it is an essential tool for understanding site behavior.

KPIs

Companies use Key Performance Indicators (KPIs) to track the health of their business. In marketing departments, common metrics include revenue, revenue source, visits to the site, and conversions. But KPIs can be anything important to the health of the business.

KPI decks are usually accurate and they tell you a lot about what the company values most. They are also important because they provide a historical record. You can see how the metrics trend, spot seasonality, and get a feel for how well the business is performing.

One weakness is that while they tell you a lot about what the company values, they don't always tell you a lot about why customers behave the way they do. KPIs are about what has occurred and seldom about why it has occurred.

It's also worth digging into the methodology behind the KPIs. For instance, is revenue net or gross? If it's net, how was it calculated? If the company sells internationally, how did they calculate exchange rates? While the numbers are accurate they may not represent exactly what you think they do.

Site KPIs

Site KPIs track behavior from both paid and unpaid sources. If the company has tracked site KPIs over multiple years, the data can be extremely useful for developing insights into long-term audience behavior.

Common metrics include:

- Visitors: How many people have come to the site.

- Visits: The total number of times people have come to the site.

- Pageviews: How many pages people visited while on the site.

- Revenue: Generally gross. Sometimes net as well, especially if looking at revenue from marketing campaigns.

- Average Order Value: The average value of each order. For instance, if there are 10 purchases and revenue is $100, then the average order value would be $10. Note that this is the average – the actual distribution could be nine $1 purchases and one $91 purchase.

- eCommerce Rate: Number of conversions divided by the number of visits.

- Number of conversions: On eCommerce sites, a conversion is usually an order. On a site that sells products through its sales teams, a conversion can be someone submitting their contact information. People sometimes also define a conversion as a user action, for example when a user downloads a white paper.

Companies track metrics broken out by source so they can spot areas that are profitable and areas that are struggling. Companies will often place the KPIs for paid traffic and unpaid traffic in separate sections. Businesses can see how well the site is performing through unpaid channels and analyze return on investment for paid marketing efforts.

Sources that are often tracked:

- All sources (combined)
- Unpaid:
    - Organic: Visits that come from search engines such as Google.
    - Direct: Visits by people who follow a bookmarked link or type in the URL. In some analytics systems, visits that can't be attributed to a source are included in the direct traffic. Typically direct traffic is the most engaged traffic with the highest conversion rate.
    - Referral: Visits by people who clicked a link that took them to your site.
- Paid:
    - Email: Email campaigns to drive new or recurring business.

- SEM (Search Engine Marketing): Ads that appear in search results, for example on Google.
- Paid social media: For instance, ads placed on Facebook.
- Other paid channels

Companies track different KPIs depending on their business and focus. For instance, some companies also track the purchase funnel steps, top pages, metrics by location, revenue broken out by currency, or average number of items in an order. The data points companies track depend on the types of questions they want to answer.

Competitive analysis

Competitive analysis identifies competitors and analyzes how they are positioned against your company. Among other information, a competitive analysis will look at competitor strengths and weaknesses relative to your own.

Depending on resources, competitive analysis can range from an informal PowerPoint presentation to intensive, ongoing research.

Competitive analysis is important for understanding how to position a company online and make the most compelling pitch possible to users. Companies use competitive analysis information to make the most out of their strengths and to avoid pitfalls that competitors could exploit.

When reviewing competitors, it's worth taking a look at their websites in detail. A few questions to get you started:

- What do their user personas look like?
- How do they assume users will move through the site?
- Which site decisions are based on what the user wants? Which are based on what the company wants?

Figuring out the answers to these questions requires some intuitive leaps. By studying a competitor's site, though, you can deduce a lot of this information if the site is well built.

Your competitors have likely solved similar problems to the ones you need to solve, so looking at their sites can spark useful observations and questions.

The biggest strength of competitive analysis is that it gives you insight into the landscape you'll be competing in. You know the key competitors and their strengths and weaknesses. You may also get ideas about what to highlight on your own site.

The biggest weakness is that competitive analysis is often full of internal assumptions that can skew results and give you misleading information.

Many small companies haven't run a competitive analysis. You may need to collect notes on your own.

Companies solving similar problems

As well as looking at competitors' sites, look at sites that have solved problems similar to the ones you need to solve.

Examine sites that are not in direct competition or even the same industry. By looking outside your immediate competitors, you'll find good ideas and approaches that will set you apart.

For instance, suppose you sell a large number of items divided over multiple categories. You need to get ideas for how to display information. You might look at Etsy, the Apple App Store, and MyFonts for inspiration. These are in different lines of business, but they all have huge numbers of products. So one, or all of them, might have useful ideas to add to your observations.

To be clear, I'm not advising that you copy other sites, but rather that you understand why their solutions work and to learn from those principles. If you understand the principles you can develop ideas for your own site.

The biggest strength with this approach is that you can breathe fresh life into your site. By researching across multiple industries, you'll get a new perspective on how to solve problems.

The biggest weakness is that you can spend a lot of time researching something that isn't useful. It requires practice to get this right.

Customer service

Customer service is a good source of information. Discussions with customer service agents about customer motivations and pain points can be useful as they talk to customers all the time.

Most customer service departments track the topics of the questions and complaints they receive. This can be very helpful. For instance, if customer service receives a lot of questions about the return policy, it might be worth making the link to the return policy more prominent on the site.

It's also worth taking a look at the tickets. By reviewing the tickets, you can get insight into user concerns and discover important edge cases.

The great strength of customer service is that they talk to customers constantly and have a deep knowledge of customer motivations and frustrations.

They can also act as an early warning system if a site change is going badly. Customer service often hears about issues before they are caught anywhere else.

The biggest weakness is that the information can be anecdotal and customer service is not necessarily talking to the typical customer. They are often talking to customers who are grumpy or frustrated or just plain confused. So their views may tend toward the negative. They may give too much weight to the complaints of a few noisy customers.

A/B and multivariate testing

In its simplest form, A/B testing is comparing the original version of a page (the control) against a modified version to see which one performs better. Multivariate testing is a more complicated set up but the core idea is the same.

When you run a test, you see how a change performs on a live site with an audience. Since you run the test version against a control, you can compare the two versions and observe the impact of the changes. This saves a lot of internal discussion because you can tell which version performs better.

When reviewing historical test results, the main strength is that you can see how the audience reacted to a change. With this information you can sometimes deduce a lot about the audience.

A major weakness of testing is that poorly set-up tests can give misleading results. The test documentation may also be incomplete. This makes it difficult to understand what was tested, why and what the results meant.

An often overlooked weakness of testing is that the site exists in a constantly changing environment. Testing will give you a winning variation *at the time of the test*, but it may not be permanently true. If your audience's make up or motivations changed significantly since the test was run, what tested well previously may no longer produce results.

Personas

Personas are fictional characters that represent users. The persona humanizes the user, making it easier to design for or market to the customer.

Ideally a persona is built after intensive research. The more thorough the research, the more accurate the persona. Personas can include information about gender, age, motivations, challenges, and goals.

Different departments often have different personas. For instance, the marketing team and the product team will likely have different personas.

The main advantage of personas is that, done well, they can be incredibly helpful. They tell you about your customers and who will be using the site. They may even tell you about their goals and motivations.

The main disadvantage of personas is a subtle one. It won't trip everyone up, but it can lead to bad choices. Personas portray users as individuals. That's why they work – because it's easier to think about what an individual would want rather than an undefined user. But by assigning traits to the user, you tap into subconscious assumptions, for example about age, gender and race. By defining these characteristics, people can make incorrect assumptions that they are not aware of but that influence their decisions.

When you define a persona with specific characteristics, you also remove people who don't have those characteristics. This can lead to blind spots in how you talk to or design for your audience.

Another disadvantage in many small companies is that people have a hard time constructing personas. Teams are often also contentious about their accuracy and the personas are not used or kept up to date.

Positioning statement

There are a few different flavors of positioning statements, but in general they describe the target audience, the unique value a company delivers, and how that company is differentiated from its competitors. In other words, who is going to buy from you and why.

These are incredibly useful when they're well done. If you work for a small company and a positioning statement does not exist, consider working with the marketing department to create one.

Existing theories

Every company has them. The ideas people pass around about why customers behave the way they do and what it means for the business.

If the theories are based on solid evidence, they can be useful. This is especially true if the evidence is recent.

If they're just opinions, they can still be useful but treat them with caution. Usually they have a grain or two of truth in them, but it takes a little digging to get to those grains.

Add existing theories to your observations, but treat them with a fair amount of skepticism.

Best practices

Best practices include ideas such as how much information to put on a page, where to place the call to action buttons, and how to keep users moving in the purchase flow. If you are not familiar with best practices, spend some time researching them. There are many excellent resources available on this topic.

Make sure you understand *why* the best practices work. If you understand why, you'll have a better sense of when to use them and how to adapt them.

Knowing best practices makes it easier to find places where the site can be improved. However, they can vary by audience and site so be thoughtful in how you apply them.

Additional research

Gathering existing information is a good first step. The next step, though, is to fill in the gaps. If there is important information missing you may need to partner with other teams or run the research yourself. The more information you can gather at this stage, the stronger your conclusions will be in later steps.

As well as running additional research, cross-check data against other sources to find inconsistencies. For instance, a focus group tells you that your customers love online chat and use it regularly. When you pull the numbers, though, you see that customers rarely use online chat. This might mean that for the tiny percentage of times customers use chat it's very important to them that they can get help immediately. Or it might mean that customers value the fact they *could* chat with someone directly and it makes them feel more secure. Or it could be a data issue. Or perhaps none of these explanations is correct and you'll find the answer when you dig further into the data.

Comparing different sets of information is useful when you're sorting out what's true, what's false, and what points to a deeper user motivation.

Other

Other sources of information include, but are not limited to: social media; surveys; conversations with customers; usability testing; chatting around the water cooler with other departments; sales collateral; newsletter results; revenue reports; and industry blogs. There is often a lot of information out there if you know where to look.

Keep your eyes and ears open, and talk to anyone who seems interested in understanding user behavior. Some of the best insights can come from unexpected sources.

Degree of confidence

I've gone over many places that you can look for information. You may have noticed that some sources are more reliable than others.

For instance, an anecdotal story can be interesting and suggest new avenues for research, but is rarely justification for action on its own. Web analytics reports are not perfect but they are often reliable and useful for decision making.

In the next steps, when you start interpreting information and building questions, make sure to weigh your observations according to how reliable they are. Questions and hypotheses that are based on reliable observations are often better to pursue than those based on weaker observations.

State of mind, motivations and audience segments

As you collect information, you'll find out a lot about *what* actions users take. After awhile you'll probably start to wonder *why* users take the actions they do.

The why is endlessly interesting and makes a huge difference to the approach you take on the site. A different page will work for someone who's frustrated (for example, a simple, clear, easy-to-follow page) than for someone who is curious and motivated to learn more (for example, an information-rich page with connected content to pull visitors deeper into the site). User state of mind and user motivations influence how you should put your site together.

User state of mind and motivations are tricky to nail down and they vary across audience segments. They are also very hard to interpret with insufficient data. As you go through the Six Steps you'll gather more targeted knowledge about your audience and develop a better understanding of their state of mind and motivations.

State of mind

The users' state of mind impacts the success of a site. A site design that is sympathetic to the users' state of mind is more likely to be successful. A site design that is at odds with the audience may cause people to leave or to view the product or brand less favorably.

A good first step for getting into the user's mind is to think about how the user is likely to feel. How do users feel when they first arrive on the site? Once they're on the site, how do they react to your product? Finally, how does the site itself impact the users' emotions? Do all of these elements line up or are they discordant?

Preexisting emotional state

It's easy to think of users as a blank slate. However, they usually arrive on a site with a whole set of predefined ideas and emotions.

For instance, if you're building a support section, people may arrive stressed and frustrated. The support site should be calming with a clear path funneling people to the answers they need. If they're already exasperated, you don't want to further frustrate them by making it hard to find an answer.

They may also have a state of mind that has nothing to do with your product or site directly.

If your site sells practical items with no strong inherent emotional charge (for example, dish soap), people may be in a rush. They want to get a chore done and are impatient to complete the transaction as quickly as possible. Their reaction is unrelated to the product and the site, but the site needs to help them with the maximum of ease and minimum of aggravation.

Look at what causes the preexisting emotional state and how it impacts user behavior on the site. If you're fortunate, you'll have reliable evidence about the users' preexisting emotional state. More likely, you will have to infer it based on what you know.

Emotional charge of the product or service

People have strong, and sometimes not wholly acknowledged, reactions to products. Understanding how your product is likely to impact a user's emotional state will influence the approach you take with the site.

For instance, money is often a source of stress. If a company sells personal financial software, a low-key site with a reserved font and carefully doled out information might be very effective. Users will feel reassured and comforted by a calming environment.

On the other hand, if your site sells luxury items, users may come in with the idea of indulging themselves and so they want to linger over your site. The shopping experience is part of the satisfaction. The whole site experience should meet this emotional need, for instance with gorgeous pictures, stunning typography, lovingly written descriptions and elegant product names.

When thinking about emotional charge, consider the product

from a user's perspective. If the user knew nothing about the company, how would they react to the site? Then think about how branding and marketing influences the user's opinion. Finally, are there any social considerations that will impact the user's view? Surveys and user interviews may surface useful insights into emotional charge.

Impact of the site

The site influences the users' state of mind.

The mechanics of the site can shift the users' emotional response. If your site makes users feel unnecessarily anxious or, worse yet, dumb you will lose revenue. Well-documented sources of anxiety include poorly defined return policies, confusing purchase flows, and jumbled site hierarchy.

The feel of the site can also impact users. Image choices, typography and other design elements can send signals to users. For instance, a site that sells clothes to men and women but has a "feminine" feel may prompt men to leave without knowing why. If the indicators you use suggest that some of your customers are not welcome, they probably won't hang around.

Consider how the site design may be impacting the users' state of mind.

Motivations

Motivations drive people to make decisions. Motivations are extremely important to figure out but they are often hard to pin down.

Surface motivations reflect a stated, often rational goal. *Fundamental motivations* are not always conscious. They are motivations that exist at an instinctual or emotional level.

Let's look at how surface and fundamental motivations could play out:

Peter decides to buy a designer laptop bag. If you asked Peter why he bought the bag, he might say something like 'I need a bag to carry my laptop around in and these bags look great'. This is most likely true and it reflects surface motivations.

But Peter has another unstated, but fundamental, motivation: Status. The smartest, hippest people Peter works with all have this designer laptop bag, and he is using the bag as a sign that he fits in with that social circle. The bag is a representation of status and, potentially, connection with other people he sees as high status.

While Peter would tell you that he is buying the bag because it looks great, he makes the purchase because he wants to fit in with a high-status social circle at work.

People are typically comfortable discussing surface motivations as they are logical and obvious. However, they are not always consciously aware of fundamental motivations and can be uncomfortable or embarrassed discussing them. Fundamental motivations often show up indirectly.

Surface motivations

Marketers talk about features versus benefits. Features are the factual statements of what a product offers; benefits are what advantage the product confers. For instance, if you were marketing software for building websites, a feature might be 100s of site templates. The benefit is that you can customize your site to look however you want it to.

Almost always, promoting benefits outperforms promoting features.

Surface motivations line up well with benefits. They're the motivations you can state directly and that answers what's in it for the customer. To return to the example of Peter, a company could market the laptop bag as practical and attractive.

Surface motivations are an important part of a high-achieving site and you need to have them firmly locked down. But they skate on top of fundamental motivations. If you understand the fundamental motivations, it's easier to get the surface motivations right and determine what's getting your customers to respond to your product.

Fundamental motivations

As with state of mind, fundamental motivations require some guesswork. The user isn't always aware of them so you can't just ask.

There are many different models that explain why people behave as they do. Psychology and evolutionary biology are both interesting places to look for models.

Because this can be a challenging topic, I've pulled together examples of fundamental motivations. You will probably need to add to this list, but to get started:

Status

Humans are social creatures and status within a social group is a strong motivator. Marketers often take advantage of this when they're building a brand, especially a luxury one. A product can confer status directly. For example, an expensive brand name pair of shoes can be a status signifier. A product can also indirectly confer status. For example, if a product improves the user's work performance, it could improve his status. The user does a better job with the help of the product and gets a promotion. The product improves the user's status even though the product is not a status marker.

Connection

Related to status, connection is about how we connect and build relationships with others. Social connection is one of the big drivers for social networks. Connections motivate people to join a social network and keep them coming back. It is also connected to altruism. For instance, a user's feeling that they are connected to other people can help motivate donations to non-profits.

Self-expression

Individuals need to distinguish themselves from others and have their own identity. Self-expression can drive private actions and motivate social behavior. For instance, self-expression motivates people to write in journals (a private action) and on blogs (a social behavior). When self-expression is a social behavior, it is often related to connection and status.

Attractiveness

People buy products they believe will "directly" make them more attractive, e.g. clothes, or will "magically" make them more attractive, e.g. by drinking a specific beer. People also enjoy looking at attractive people and this compels attention, a strategy summed up as "sex sells".

Resource conservation

People are often careful how they use resources. The obvious example is saving money, i.e. a stored resource, so discounts and coupons generate business. People also usually don't want to use more effort than they need to. For instance if your site is hard to navigate or your product offering is hard to understand, then, unless the expected reward is very high, they are likely to just leave. In this case they're conserving mental effort and time. People are very good at minimizing mental resource use.

Pain avoidance

People avoid painful situations. Pain avoidance is a commonly used tactic in marketing. For example, retirement planning ads that ask, 'Have you saved enough for retirement?'. These ads use anxiety and the fear of future pain. There is also a more subtle variant of this. If your site is painful to use because it is difficult or it makes people feel dumb, people will stay away from it.

Audience segments

So far I've discussed state of mind and user motivations as if they are consistent for everyone who comes to a site. The truth is much more complicated. User state of mind and motivations can vary significantly across different audience groups.

Think about the different groups of people who might visit your site. Obvious groups include people who want to make a purchase or current customers who visit the homepage to log in. But your audience also includes less obvious groups such as job seekers and investors.

Within these larger groups are subgroups. Customers who make an expensive purchase can behave differently than ones who make an inexpensive purchase. The site may market to both consumers and businesses. It may market to professionals and hobbyists. These groups all behave differently.

Once you have listed the groups, think about what individuals in each group want to accomplish and why. How can the site help them accomplish their goals?

Then look at which audience groups have the most impact on your goals. For instance, if you need to increase revenue, look at which groups contribute the highest levels of revenue.

Getting a good view into your audience segments makes it easier to build an effective site with well-prioritized information and features.

Chapter summary

- Collect observations to base decisions on. Decisions based on evidence are more likely to be successful.

- You can find a lot of information just by looking. Sources include site data, competitive research and websites of companies solving similar problems.

- All sources have weaknesses; some are more reliable than others.

- Typically when you gather observations you'll find information about *what* users do, but not as much about *why* users act as they do. The *why* is an important question to answer. You need to understand audience behavior and predict what the audience will respond well to. Digging into user state of mind and motivations helps answer the *why*.

- When thinking about users' state of mind, consider their preexisting emotional state and the emotional impact of your offer and site.

- One way to think about motivations is to break them into two groups – those that are at a conscious, surface level and those that are fundamental. The surface level motivations line up with the marketing concept of benefits. Fundamental motivations have their roots in human needs, such as a need to connect with others, to be self-expressive, to avoid pain. The line between surface and fundamental motivations can be hazy.

- Each audience segment is likely to have a different combination of state of mind and motivations.

Observations:

Susan recently started working at the Fancy Cake Company. She composed and received executive approval on the site objective:

"Increase revenue generated by the Fancy Cake Company website by 50% over the next 12 months."

Susan collected observations and did some additional research on her own. Her observations are extensive but there are a few key ones.

The main audience groups are consumers (B2C), businesses (B2B), and the artisan bakeries that sell products through the Fancy Cake Company site.

B2C accounts for most of the site revenue. This revenue

stays largely consistent throughout the year, though there is an increase around the holidays and in the summer months.

The B2B revenue is mostly generated by businesses sending out holiday gifts to clients and associates. 80% of business revenue is generated in just two months.

The artisan bakers produce the product rather than buy it. They are an important audience group as, without them, the site won't succeed. This part of the business is looking healthy. There is a high retention rate of bakeries and significant numbers of new artisan bakeries have applied to join the site.

Originally, the Fancy Cake Company produced and sold all of the baked goods on the site. The Fancy Cake Company still has its own line of baked goods, but other artisan bakeries now produce most of the baked goods sold on the site.

The Fancy Cake Company worked with three of its top bakeries to offer a free cupcake with every cake purchase when customers used the promo code FREE. The promotion ran from November 15 to November 28, and was only promoted through email. Susan wonders if this impacted site behavior. She takes a look at what terms people used when searching on the site. She filters the internal search site queries by the word "free" and finds that very few people entered the promo code into search.

However, the word "free" appeared in many of the queries. Susan analyzes the queries and finds that people often search for dairy free, gluten free and nut free. She mentions this to customer service and they report that they get the occasional call about allergens in the cakes.

Customer service also mentions that the most common question callers ask is whether the Fancy Cake Company offers cakes for specific occasions. Birthday and wedding cakes are most often asked about. The second most common question is whether it's possible to order a custom cake.

Susan researches other sites including one that sells computer bags. She visits because she wants to study the information architecture, but while there she notices a "build a bag" tool. The tool catches her attention as it is fun to use. It is also a compelling way to engage with customers and encourage additional sales.

During her research Susan notices that sites that are in a similar space to the Fancy Cake Company have large, attractive pictures that show off the food in detail.

Susan also looks at the traffic sources for the site. A decent percentage of visits comes through search engines such as Google and from referrals. She also sees a significant number of direct visits, i.e. people who typed in FancyCakeCompany.com or who had bookmarked a page. When Susan has a look at the landing pages for direct traffic, many go to specific product pages and not to a more general page like the homepage.

Susan gives some thought to the state of mind and motivations of her audience.

For the B2B segment it appears straightforward. The main motivation seems to be finding a unique and interesting gift that is easy to order in large numbers for delivery to multiple businesses throughout the US. This behavior is tied to the end of the year gift-giving season. The reason companies send cakes as gifts may be that they are memorable, non-controversial, and appeal to most people. This is speculation, but fits with what is known.

For the B2C segment, it's more complicated. Susan looks through focus group results, site behavior data and competitor sites. She comes to a few tentative conclusions. It seems likely that customers who come to the site like the experience of buying a small-batch baked good that feels special. They support small businesses over large corporations, both from a philosophical point of view and because it matches their sense of self. She suspects they often share the baked goods with others, reinforcing their social position. Since the price point is high for baked goods, it seems likely that they are well off.

Step 3: Questions

You've identified the problem you need to solve, gathered your observations and now questions are bubbling up in your mind. You probably see some connections between your observations but also some inconsistencies.

In this step create as many question as you can – big, small, important, inconsequential, it doesn't matter. What starts off as a small thread can turn into a very big insight. Because you don't have all the information yet, it's hard to know what will be important.

Ground rules

Before you start creating questions, there are a few ground rules. By following these ground rules, your questions are more likely to be successful.

Be honest

Your data is not always going to tell you what you want it to tell you. It will be bad news sometimes. Being honest about the bad news can be tough, but it's worth it.

When you are honest with yourself, you make better decisions.

When you are honest with co-workers, you build a reputation for trustworthiness. It will occasionally mean delivering bad news. In the long term, though, it will be easier to carry the points that are important to you. People will know you're presenting accurate information to justify your decisions.

Be curious

A constant need to know why and to know more will drive your research better than anything else. If you don't accept the obvious surface explanations and keep digging you can find out a lot about users and their motivations. With this knowledge you will make better decisions for the site.

It's also fun to dig below the surface. You can discover another question and another new insight that fits into the larger picture evolving in your mind.

Be humble

Don't try to know more than you do. The goal is not to be right immediately. It's to make the smartest changes for the site.

If you go in assuming you already know everything, you'll probably only notice information that confirms what you already believe.

If you go in assuming that you have a lot to learn, you are more likely to notice useful but unexpected information.

Be skeptical

Being skeptical is one of the best ways to ensure your data and conclusions will be accurate.

Be skeptical of your data and your data sources. Compare multiple sources of information to look for discrepancies. When you find them, figure out the source of the inconsistency.

Be skeptical of your conclusions. No one is always right and the unexpected errors are the hardest to spot. Try to prove yourself wrong.

All this can be painful. But by being skeptical, your conclusions will be much more accurate and therefore more effective. And in the end that is what you want.

Creating questions

We'll take a look at two types of thinking and then review a method for creating questions.

Convergent and divergent thinking

When looking at data, there are two general approaches to take.

The first is convergent thinking. Convergent thinking arrives at a "correct" answer to a clear-cut question.

The second is divergent thinking, a creative process in which you create many possible answers to a question.

Most people are reasonably good at convergent thinking because schools typically train for it with standardized tests. Divergent thinking can take a little more practice.

Convergent thinking

You use convergent thinking when answering standard questions that have a single correct answer. For instance, convergent thinking is used for filling out spreadsheets of key performance indicators (KPIs), whether they're data points for a newsletter, an ad campaign or a website.

A question to prompt convergent thinking could look like: "What is the site's eCommerce rate this month?". A company might calculate this for a regular report. There is only one correct answer to the question each month.

You also use convergent thinking when you make a simple deduction. When you make deductions, the goal is to reduce the number of possibilities rather than expand them.

Divergent thinking

Divergent thinking is more difficult and time-consuming than convergent thinking, but also more interesting and fun. When using this approach, the questions you ask can be big or small and are open ended.

A question to prompt divergent thinking could look like: "Why is the site's eCommerce rate 1% this month?". The question is open ended and may have multiple answers. Is it tied to changes in traffic? Is the 1% conversion rate because of a site change? Is it because there's a decrease in orders from overseas? Is it because competitors launched new features and the company is no longer keeping up?

When the news is bad, you can come up with ideas to fix the problem. When the news is good, you can find ways to build on your success.

When you use divergent thinking you develop insights into your audience. Combining information in new and interesting ways leads to surprisingly insightful ideas.

Upshot

Both convergent and divergent thinking are important.

Answering predefined questions is necessary if you're building a KPI deck or making a simple deduction. As long as the questions are smart, the data is useful.

But if you're trying to understand user behavior, employing divergent thinking is much more effective. It's harder because it takes more creativity and intuition, but it can drive breakthroughs in understanding.

Because divergent thinking is open ended, it is well suited for creating questions and for the first stages of hypothesis building.

Method

Expect to create many questions – big questions, small questions, nagging questions about data that doesn't make sense, and anything else on your mind. The more questions you can create the better.

Organizing your observations into a table can be helpful when forming questions. The table should contain three columns:

- **Observations:** In this column, place the information you have gathered. You may need to be selective about what information you include.

- **Deductions:** This column contains the simplest deductions. Ideas that are well supported by the facts you've gathered. To create these, you use convergent thinking. You'll combine what you learn from your deductions with observations to create questions.

- **Questions:** This column lists speculative ideas. They're ideas that you don't have enough information to verify, but that you can research further. You use divergent thinking to arrive at these questions. The questions form the basis for the next step, creating hypotheses.

An example of a filled-in table:

<table>
<tr><th>Observations</th><th>Deductions</th><th>Questions</th></tr>
<tr><td>Unexpected 5% decrease in step 3 to 4 of the purchase funnel from June 3rd on</td><td rowspan="2">The new billing system may be causing the decrease.</td><td rowspan="2">5% means the issue is fairly uncommon. What tests do we need to run to find the issue? Are we still accepting all credit cards? All currencies? Are users timing out? Are there browser-specific issues?</td></tr>
<tr><td>New billing system put in place on June 3rd</td></tr>
</table>

A small number of internal site search terms are product-specific rather than general (e.g. "Arizona Bakery Short Sweet Shortcake" versus "Shortcake")	Search on the site is important. Make sure that search results are accurate, give users a clear next step, and are easy to understand.	• Are people pre-researching before they buy? If so, how and where? • Are these repeat customers who are buying the same product each time? • Individuals or businesses? What is this group's average order size? Do they send the cake to themselves or to other people? • Would putting up cross sells after a product-specific search increase, decrease or make no difference to revenue? • What is the quality of search results for general terms? Are the results returning the information the users are looking for?
Users who do a site search with a product-specific term are much more likely to make a purchase than users who search on general terms		
Customers who used a product-specific search term on the site account for 30% of the revenue		

The table above is a simple one. Yours may be more complex. For instance, you'll have more observations. Some of your observations will be inconsistent with one another. You may also decide to exclude unreliable or less relevant observations.

By structuring your observations, deductions and questions you will be able to refer to your previous ideas, pull existing information together and add in new layers of information. Your questions will be smarter, more focused, and you'll learn more with less effort.

Common themes

If you're not sure where to start with questions, knowing common themes can help you think about the types of questions to ask.

These themes follow a common framework:

- Is the site meeting the company's goals? (Company Goals)
- Is the site addressing the audience's goals? (Audience Goals)
- What do you want the audience to do next and how easy are you making it? (Usability)

I've also found these themes to be important:

- Data shifts caused by internal and external events (What Changed?)
- Information that seems important but it's not immediately clear why (Intuition)

These are useful themes to examine, but each project has unique needs and challenges. You'll want to create your own list.

Let's look at each theme in more detail.

Company goals

A site is a collection of pages and sections that should work together to support the company's goals.

As a first step identify the key areas of the site. Then assess if they are supporting company goals. You can identify key pages in a couple of ways:

- *Look at the pages with the most traffic.* High traffic areas could be a single page, such as the homepage, or a combined group of pages, such as all search results pages. The advantage of this approach is that you look at pages based on how users are interacting with your site. Ideally, your users are telling you what they care about by which pages they visit. Looking at the most popular pages can also show you where users are heading off in the wrong direction or searching for important information they cannot find.

- *Study the pages you would expect users to visit.* For a customer on an eCommerce site, that might include the homepage, product listings, product page and purchase funnel. The advantage of this approach is that it includes important pages even if they don't get much traffic. For instance, pages in the purchase funnel usually don't get much traffic relative to the rest of the site, but these pages are important.

Once you've identified the key pages think about whether they support company goals:

- How did the people who created the site expect users to interact with it? You may be able to ask or you may have to deduce the answer.
- Then look at the data. How are users interacting with the site?
- How do the answers to both these questions line up with the goals of the site?

Let's walk through an example to get a better feel for this.

Nisa works for a company that markets site-blocking software. When the software is in place, users can only visit approved websites. Parents who want to limit their kids' Internet access are the main buyers of this software, but the company wants to expand the business side. Businesses can use the software to limit the sites employees visit.

Nisa identifies the business section as a set of key pages. The business section launched to great fanfare. The site builders' intent was that business users would visit and purchase from that section.

Nisa discovers that while the business section is receiving a fair amount of traffic, almost no one is making a purchase from those pages.

Nisa answers the questions above:

- *How did the people who created the site expect the users to interact with it?*

  They expected business visitors to visit the business section and make a purchase

- *How are users interacting with the site?*

  They're visiting the section but are not making a purchase

- *How do the answers to both these questions line up with the goals of the site?*

  As the goal is to increase business purchases, the business section is not supporting the goals of the site.

So the big question Nisa has to answer is why are the pages not converting? To answer this, Nisa may look at the effectiveness of the page, the product offering and the competitive landscape.

Audience goals

Company and audience goals need to line up. A company can have any goal it wants, but the company will only be successful if the audience's actions support that goal. For instance, a company might have a goal to make money through the sales of a product. But that goal will only be achieved if the audience buys the product.

Review the site through the eyes of each audience segment. Does the site support the goals and motivations of each audience group? If not, where are the problems and how can they be solved?

Usability

As you looked at whether the site aligned with company and audience goals, you probably found usability issues. How easy is the site to use and navigate and what challenges does the visitor face?

The source of many usability issues is that the people who created the site become too familiar with it. They lose perspective on how complex the site is for someone who's new to it.

A common usability issue is that the visitor is not sure what the next step is after visiting a page. If the call to action is not present or prominent, the visitor may simply leave.

Providing far too much information or information arranged in a way that's hard to follow is also a common problem. Partially this is because it is a balancing act. People need enough information to make a decision but they are easily overwhelmed. And different audience segments need different information at different times. This makes it hard to show the correct amount of information. Sometimes, though, the problem is the company's inability to self-edit.

Making users work too hard also creates usability issues. For instance, using terminology users are not familiar with or expecting them to provide more than a minimum amount of information in the purchase flow.

There are many good books about site usability and information architecture. I've mentioned a smattering of usability issues, but it is an area that repays further study.

What changed?

Look at how a change in the environment impacts site behavior, revenue and other important metrics. By analyzing how a change in the environment impacts user behavior, you can gain insight into audience motivations.

Seasonality is a common environmental change. For instance, look at audience motivations for what people buy and why at the holidays. Does your audience change at this time of year? How can you accomodate them?

On the flip side, knowing that revenue typically drops every June because that's when your customers take their yearly vacation will save you a few headaches. You may be able to develop strategies that combat the seasonal downturn.

Other sources of change include pricing adjustments, the competitive landscape, demographic shifts, marketing pushes, and site changes.

Looking at what changed is valuable because it shakes up assumptions. When you only see the status quo, you don't know if your assumptions are right or wrong. If your ideas about user behavior are correct, then the change will have a predictable outcome. If your ideas are incorrect, then the outcome will be unpredictable. Catching incorrect assumptions is useful as it helps you develop questions and refine your ideas. The more accurate your ideas, the more likely your site changes are to work.

Intuition

Intuition taps you on the shoulder and asks you to pay attention to things that don't immediately make sense. When something first feels off or important, it's not always clear why. Often it is just a feeling of wrongness about a data point, a minor inconsistency that nags, that will drive you to look further into what's going on.

Once you pull that thread and see what unravels, you can get a whole new understanding of the situation.

Intuition has a bad name for a good reason – people abuse it. They use intuition to throw out solutions to problems rather than thinking with the result that the solutions fail. Don't do that. Intuition is valuable as long as you use it as a starting point, not as a solution. Follow up on your ideas to understand what's going on.

Chapter summary

- Expect to create many questions, big and small. You'll narrow them down later, but at this step you want breadth and creativity.

- When creating questions there are a few ground rules that will help you be successful: be honest, curious, humble and skeptical.

- Convergent thinking arrives at a “correct” answer to a clear-cut question. A typical example is the answer to “How many people visited the site in May?”.

- Divergent thinking requires creativity. You develop many different ideas when you use divergent thinking. An example of a question that could lead to divergent thinking is “How can we get more people to visit the site?”.

- When creating questions, pull together multiple observations and make simple deductions with convergent thinking. Then use divergent thinking to create a series of questions with your observations and deductions as the starting point.

- Questions often group around the themes of company goals, audience goals, site usability, impact of change, and intuition. However, this varies across projects and projects may have additional groupings.

Questions

Susan, who works at the Fancy Cake Company, has been tasked with increasing site revenue. She has collected observations and is ready to make connections and derive insights.

Susan pulls together a table with observations, deductions and questions:

Observations	**Deductions**	**Questions**
Main revenue driver: B2C	B2C may be the best segment to focus on to increase revenue	How can we increase revenue from the B2C segment?
Secondary revenue driver: B2B		
B2B sales are mostly at the end of the year	Appears to be business gift giving	Would upsells to more expensive cakes work?
People often search on the site for allergen information	Allergen information is an important piece of information for an unknown percentage of the audience	Would surfacing allergen information, for example through filters, increase sales?
Customer support reports that they receive allergen questions regularly		
Customer support says that people often call in to ask about cakes for special occasions	Special occasion cakes are of interest to a subset of the audience	Can we increase revenue by changing the information architecture to include special occasions? Should we promote special occasion cakes in the newsletters?
There is no special occasion category or filter on the site		

Customers call in to request customized cakes	Some customers are interested in modifying cakes to fit their own tastes / needs better	Would a “build your own cake” tool be fun? profitable? set us apart from future competitors?
An unrelated site had a fun “build a bag” tool		
Sites that sell premade food often have large, attractive pictures of the food	The owners of these sites likely believe the large attractive pictures help sell the product	Is this something to try on Fancy Cake Company? Would it increase revenue?
People are bookmarking and returning to specific product pages	Make sure the links are stable	How many sales are connected to this user behavior? Are they repeat customers or people who did research earlier and are coming back to the page?

This table lists only a subset of Susan’s observations and deductions.

Step 4: Hypotheses

The first part of the Six Steps is about understanding the business and the environment it exists in and then using questions to find areas of opportunity.

Now that you've done the foundational work, you need to decide which ideas you want to pursue and which you want to shelve.

The ideas you decide to pursue will be your hypotheses.

Elements of a hypothesis

The easiest way to think about a hypothesis is as a short story that predicts user behavior when a variable is introduced.

A variable is the change you introduce to create an effect. Ideally, when you run a test you can attribute any effects you see to the variable. For instance, if your site uses blue buttons you might predict that users are more likely to sign up for a free trial if you use green buttons instead. The color of the buttons is the variable.

For site work, the building blocks of a hypothesis include:

- Area or functionality
- Variable
- Why
- Metric being tracked
- Predicted outcome

Let's dig into the building blocks in more detail.

Area or functionality

The area or functionality can be quite diverse. For instance, it could be a specific page, a repetitive user action such as saving a picture, or even an entire site.

Make sure you define the area or functionality clearly. If you do not define this clearly, you will find it difficult to construct a testable hypothesis. In fact, the more you narrow it down, the better.

Variable

A variable is a change that will create an effect.

A variable could be the color of a button, the placement of "save", the amount of information on a page, the positioning of an image, or any number of other changes.

A precise variable makes it easier to analyze the audience's reaction.

For instance, suppose you change the title on the homepage to focus on a new benefit. If you see an increase in revenue, you would gain a specific insight into what your audience responds well to.

Now suppose you move from an information-dense homepage to an information-light homepage, and your audience responds well to the new page. This one variable encompasses multiple changes so the cause of your audience's reaction is not clear. Is it because you removed information that users didn't like? Or is it because users have an easier time engaging with the content because there's less of it? Or maybe users are spending less time distracted by the homepage and reach the product pages more quickly?

A broader variable means that you can move more quickly but your results are less precise. A more tightly defined variable means you move more slowly but you know exactly what the audience is reacting to. When deciding on a variable you need to keep this trade off in mind.

A common approach is to use a broad variable (e.g. a new homepage) and then test incrementally to refine once you have a winning version (e.g. test multiple versions of the call to action button). However, the approach you take with your variables will depend on your circumstances and goals.

Why

What do you think introducing the variable will do? Predict what impact the site change will have on users and why.

Thinking through why the variable will impact your audience helps keep you honest. It's easy to think a variable is important because of politics or a particularly noisy customer. These are distractions. The audience's reaction will determine whether the change is important.

Predicting why the hypothesis will work is an important part of constructing a hypothesis. Thinking through why the change will work is an early, easy test of the validity of your hypothesis. If you can't say why it will work, there's probably something wrong with the hypothesis.

Metrics

How will you know you're right? What metrics can you measure that will show whether the change was successful?

In theory you could have multiple metrics. In practice, it's most effective to test for one metric and to keep an eye on other metrics to make sure you understand any secondary effects.

Predicted outcome

Predicted outcome is easily the area of most guesswork in

hypothesis building. It is the exception rather than the rule that you will accurately predict the impact of a site change. After all, if you could predict it accurately, you wouldn't need to run a test.

However, a predicted outcome will help you prioritize your hypotheses. A predicted outcome can also be useful when you need to get support from others for your site changes.

Some of the factors you'll want to consider when thinking about predicted outcomes:

- Audience volume
- Relationship to the site objective
- How much the change impacts the user experience
- Why you believe the change will work

Let's look at an example. The site you're working on sells a monthly subscription to an online art tool. You want to change the purchase flow from five pages to one and remove unnecessary information gathering. The goal, as stated in the site objective, is to increase sales.

- Audience Volume: Low as most people never make it to the purchase flow.

- Relationship to the site objective: Strong. If more people make it through the purchase flow, then the site will generate more sales. Even a modest improvement will create a relatively large increase in the number of sales.

- Impact: The impact on audience experience is likely to be intermediate. For some people it will make a big difference. The people who are less motivated will be much more likely to make a purchase after the change. The more enthusiastic audience members, though, are already willing to deal with barriers and they will probably make purchases at the same rate.

- Why: The current experience is not user friendly. A purchase flow that is difficult to complete increases user anxiety, making visitors more likely to leave the site. Making the purchase flow easier to use will increase sales.

You estimate a 15% improvement in sales. This is an educated guess based on what you know about the site, the audience and the environment.

As part of pulling together the predicted outcome, run a series of possible outcomes. In this case, the predicted outcome is 15%. You could run the numbers for -5%, 5%, 10%, 15% and 20% to see the range of results.

The predicted outcome is an educated guess, but it helps you identify the changes that could make the biggest difference.

Example

Let's walk through an example of how to build a hypothesis.

Having looked over the data, competitors' sites, sites that are not directly in competition with the business, etc., you decide the home page is weak. It has a lot of information, including internal jargon. It confuses visitors and they leave the site without signing up for the product.

- Area: The area you want to test is the home page.
- Variable: You want to simplify the information on the page.
- Why: You are making this change because you believe your audience will respond better to a simpler, easier-to-understand page. The homepage will no longer overwhelm the audience and the audience will be more likely to stay on the site and sign up for the product.
- Metric: The metric is the number of people who sign up for the product. Based on the traffic through the page and its current state, you expect a 5–20% improvement in conversions, which you estimate at 12% in the hypothesis.
- Hypothesis: Simplifying and streamlining the information on the home page will improve overall conversions by 12%.

Moving from questions to a hypothesis

Moving from a set of questions to a hypothesis sounds easy but it requires an intuitive leap. Let's walk through an example of the process.

Site objective

Increase revenue from the website by 30% over the next 6 months.

Observations and Questions

<table>
<tr><th>Observations</th><th>Deductions</th><th>Questions</th></tr>
<tr><td>At the end of August the company changed how information is displayed on the product pages</td><td>Impact unknown</td><td>Why were these changes made? What was the predicted impact?</td></tr>
<tr><td>The average order value dropped in September and has stayed low</td><td rowspan="2">If overall revenue has stayed consistent but average order value has dropped, the number of orders has increased</td><td rowspan="2">Why did the average order value fall? Is it connected to the product page changes?</td></tr>
<tr><td>Even though average order value dropped the overall revenue has stayed consistent</td></tr>
<tr><td>In September, the marketing department started using a new newsletter format. Their click through rate went through the roof, but revenue tied to the newsletters has decreased.</td><td>The poor performance of the newsletter may be tied to the site changes or may be tied to a poor newsletter design</td><td>Is the site converting visitors from the newsletters poorly? Or is there something wrong with the newsletter? Although the newsletter encourages people to click, does it deliver low value traffic?</td></tr>
</table>

Developing hypotheses can be a multistep process that requires additional analysis. I'll discuss thought experiments more in the chapter on testing. The basic idea, though, is to look for information to confirm or invalidate your early ideas without making any audience-facing changes.

In this example, one possibility is that the site is converting low value customers much more effectively but has lost high value customers. This would create a lower average order value and more orders, but would not necessarily boost revenue.

The newsletters go out to customers who previously made a purchase. While the new newsletter format drives greater user engagement, perhaps the site is not converting the visitors into repeat customers.

Pulling the evidence together suggests the site has shifted to appeal to a different audience base. More revenue is coming from low value sales and less revenue is coming from high value sales.

While this is a consistent interpretation, there are other valid interpretations. For example, perhaps seasonality is impacting purchasing behavior. Or maybe repeat customers typically make higher value purchases and often arrive on the site through the newsletter. If the new newsletter promotes brand-building content more strongly than it promotes products, the repeat customers may not make as many purchases.

Trying to disprove your initial ideas with a thought experiment is an important step. Look for information that supports, invalidates or refines your first interpretation, and adapt your ideas as needed. If you do this, your hypotheses will have a much higher success rate.

For the sake of this example, let's say that you have dug into additional information. You are as confident as you can be without running a live test that the site is better at converting low-value purchases and poorer at converting high-value purchases.

The next step will be to build the hypothesis.

Hypothesis

As discussed there are several elements to a hypothesis:

- Area or functionality:
    - Product Pages

- Variable:
    - Information and how it is displayed on the product pages

- Why:
    - While gathering additional observations, you learn that the product pages were re-designed to be simpler. A lot of information was removed. Lower information density made the page much more user friendly, which resulted in a higher number of sales. However, cross sells to higher value products were also removed and this may have driven down the average order value.
    - The product pages appeal to customers who make inexpensive purchases. The product pages need to be re-worked to also appeal to customers who make expensive purchases.
    - The cross sells need to be added back in while maintaining a low-information density page.

- Metric being tracked:
  - Revenue

- Predicted outcome:
  - 15–20% improvement in revenue, which you estimate at 17%

Hypothesis: Improving how information is displayed on the product pages will improve revenue by 17%.

This example equates a single hypothesis with a single project. A hypothesis should test only one idea. However, you can run more than one project to test a hypothesis.

For instance, you could test the hypothesis on more than one section of the site. To expand on the example above, your hypothesis might be: "Increase the visibility of cross sells on the site to improve revenue by 20%". If this were the case, then you might run tests on the search results, the cart, and home page, as well as on the product pages. While related, these would each need to be treated as separate tests with their own predicted outcome.

When you're first starting out it can be confusing if you include multiple projects within one hypothesis. I recommend beginning with one hypothesis = one project.

Site objective (again)

Circle back to make sure the hypothesis addresses the goals in your site objective. You may find that you have been distracted by a good idea that doesn't address your goals, so this check is an important one.

The hypothesis built above passes this check as both the hypothesis and site objective focus on improving revenue.

Tips for building successful hypotheses

Now we've covered the basics of how to construct a hypothesis, here are a few ideas that will help you build a successful one.

Stay focused

The hypothesis statement needs to cover one area and one variable, and be clear about what metric (or occasionally metrics) will change and how. You should also have a good idea of why the metric will change.

If your hypothesis is unfocused, you won't get clear results.

Try to prove yourself wrong

One of the hardest things to learn when first building hypotheses is that you don't have all the answers. The assumptions you don't even realize you're making make it easy to believe that your beautiful hypothesis is a solution rather than something to test.

A hypothesis is a smart guess based on observations. While a well-formed hypothesis will make you feel like you've solved the problem, it is still nothing more than a well-educated guess.

To avoid being tripped up, embrace the possibility you could be wrong. By always admitting this possibility and actively seeking information that will prove you wrong, you'll do a better job of creating compelling and successful hypotheses.

Being wrong also has a distinct silver lining – it helps you to refine your ideas. If something didn't play out the way you expected it to, your picture of what is going on is wrong. Maybe the information you relied on was incomplete or maybe you came to an incorrect conclusion. Whichever the case, it's useful to know sooner rather than later.

No matter what the cause, if you can figure out why you were wrong, you can use that information to strengthen your hypotheses.

Remember your site objective

The site objective you formed in step one keeps you focused on the goals you are working toward. All your hypotheses should address your goals.

When you start looking through your observations, many ideas will seem interesting. If you find yourself getting off track, examine why you think a hypothesis is valuable to pursue and how it supports your site objective. In rare cases, a hypothesis that doesn't directly address your goals is worth chasing. In general, though, it's better to shelve it or pass it on to someone whose job aligns with it more closely.

Control your assumptions

Assumptions are sneaky – they're hard to spot and they mess up your thinking. The brain loves to shortcut, so it makes assumptions. The brain fits information into a preexisting mindset whenever it can.

If you think about it, this make sense. If you had to stop and re-analyze the whole situation every time something changed, you'd spend huge amounts of time and energy dealing with variations on the same situation.

Imagine if you had to relearn how to write every time you bought a different pen. It would take away a lot of flexibility. You'd only be able to use one type of pen unless you invested huge amounts of time and energy into learning how to write all over again. Instead, the mind shortcuts, finds the similarities between the new pen and previous pens, and you can write easily with the new pen.

However, the flexibility of applying old rules to new situations comes with a cost. There's a built-in assumption that because something happened a certain way in the past, or because you've been taught that something is true, it will hold true for all future situations.

Assumptions and mindsets are hard to get away from and they can be deep rooted.

For instance: Do you think people are altruistic or do you think they're solely motivated by self-interest? Do you think that people are careful or do you think they act in a rush? Do you consider individuals or think of them as numbers you can manipulate? Your answers to these types of questions can give you insight into your assumptions about people. How you think about people influences how you assume they will interact with the site and how you approach them.

There are other examples that you might not even notice. If you live in San Francisco, you might assume that most of your audience will have an up-to-date computer with a high speed internet connection because that's what you see everyday. But your audience might not be in San Francisco and they might have a different online experience.

Consider how your assumptions could impact your approach. Not only can assumptions cause you to create poor hypotheses, they can blind you to opportunities.

The good news is that if you're aware that you, like everyone else, make assumptions, you're more likely to avoid being tripped up by them.

Remember your audience

One of the best ways to prevent your assumptions from controlling you is by getting into your audience's head. Understanding as much as possible about audience motivations, state of mind and goals makes forming effective hypotheses easier. It is the audience's reaction that determines whether the site changes are successful. Consider each audience segment separately as they will all have different motivations, state of mind and goals.

At first this can feel like a lot of mental juggling as you need to consider the audience, the company goals and keep your own assumptions under control. It gets easier with practice.

Prioritization

You're likely to create many hypotheses and you'll need to decide what to work on first.

Prioritization of hypotheses works much like it does for any project. It's a matter of weighing multiple factors to decide which hypotheses take precedence.

Common factors to take into account when deciding what to prioritize are:

- Confidence
- Impact
- Risk
- Cost
- Scope
- Timeline
- Dependencies

Let's dive into the prioritization factors in more detail.

Confidence

Confidence is not usually talked about when discussing project prioritization, but it's a natural offshoot of forming hypotheses. When you create hypotheses, some of them will be well supported by evidence. Some of them will be more of a stretch.

A hypothesis well supported by observations is more likely to be successful, and so you'll have a high level of confidence in it. The more information you have to go on, the better you can refine your hypothesis and anticipate errors. The hypothesis is more precise and there are fewer variables that could upset your results. Knowing more doesn't guarantee that your hypothesis will be successful, but it makes it more likely.

A hypothesis with less data to support it is less likely to be successful, and so you'll have lower confidence in it. Your hypothesis is less trustworthy because missing information can radically change how you interpret the facts. Knowing less doesn't mean that your hypothesis will fail, but it makes it more likely.

As a general rule, more information means greater confidence in a hypothesis and less information means a lower level of confidence. Depending on risk tolerance – both personally and within the company – low or high confidence in the hypothesis can be a significant prioritization factor.

Impact

Impact is usually what first comes to mind when people think about prioritization. It's fun to think about the upside and about how much the project will help you meet business goals.

Your hypothesis should include a predicted outcome. For example, a 10% improvement in revenue. Predicted outcomes are useful because they indicate how much the change will contribute to your goals.

High-impact projects are likely to be more attractive than low-impact ones because they'll move the business forward faster.

Risk

Every site change has risks. Depending on the change, these can be quite minor all the way to very serious.

For each site change, consider unintended negative outcomes.

Unintended negative outcomes lurk in blind spots. For instance, if you update the site design so it is more modern, your customers might dislike the change. They might think the company has moved from being a Mom-and-Pop business to an untrustworthy corporate enterprise. The site is objectively better, but the change negatively impacts how customers view the company.

Before making any site change, think about what happens if it fails.

If you run an A/B test, a failing site change will probably have little impact on the company or the audience. Only a subset of the audience will have seen the test version and you can roll it back easily.

On the other hand, if you launch a new site that performs poorly it can be difficult to fix. To mitigate this, some companies run a beta version and gradually phase in the new site.

Any time you make a change, part of the plan should be how to roll back gracefully if the change fails.

There may also be political risks if the test fails. It is a good idea to intersperse the riskiest changes with safer changes. That way you can avoid a string of failures and maintain momentum.

Cost

One way to measure cost is by estimating how much money is required for a project. Common costs include buying software, contracting with specialist consultants, and hiring new permanent employees.

There are also opportunity costs. If you test your hypothesis, what other projects will be delayed and for how long? There are usually more projects than resources, so this is a common problem.

Scope

Scope is an estimate of how much work is needed to complete a project. For instance, a high scope project might be to restructure the database, which would require significant technical resources. A low scope project might be changing the hero image on the homepage, which requires very few resources.

Different teams have different approaches, but some teams assign scope by very small, small, medium, large or very large. Teams use broad categories as it's hard to predict scope perfectly. The idea is to get a sense of how many resources the project will consume.

Companies often ask developers to assign scope to their portion of the project. You will also need to consult with anyone else who will help create the site changes, e.g. designers and content producers.

Timeline

How long will it take to get the project live?

If it takes a very long time to get the project live, it may be worth skipping or adapting the project. Business needs, requirements and the competitive landscape (and therefore your site objective) might shift quickly enough that the project will no longer be relevant when it launches.

How quickly the business environment changes varies across industries and corporate cultures so this will be more important for some projects than others.

Dependencies

Dependencies between pages and sections on the site can also influence priority lists.

To create a simple example, suppose you had two projects on your list:

- Change the pricing page so it's easier to understand the different pricing tiers and what is offered at each tier.

- Fix the checkout flow so it's easier to use. The checkout flow is very poorly designed. People drop off during checkout at a rate that is significantly above industry average.

In this case, fix the checkout flow first. Only the most dedicated and determined are getting through the checkout flow. These are the people who will be least influenced by other changes on the site. They have a goal and they will complete it despite barriers.

For most users, significant obstacles like a poorly designed checkout flow will stop them from making a purchase. If you change the pricing page first, you will lose them at the checkout flow. The drop off will obscure any improvements from the new pricing page.

I've simplified the situation in this example, but the logic will hold true. A site is a collection of pages that work together. Consider dependencies between site pages and sections when building your priority list.

Be flexible

Have multiple hypotheses so you can keep moving forward even if one – or several – gets blocked.

For instance, if you suddenly find yourself with only one part-time developer instead of three full-time developers, you can move from reworking the database to redesigning the homepage. Or if you have plenty of engineering resources, but no money, you can focus on reworking the checkout flow rather than getting that new customer support system in place.

The more flexible you are, the more likely it is that you will find a successful opportunity.

If the site changes go well, it will bolster your argument for additional resources for other projects.

Chapter summary

- In this step, decide which ideas to pursue and which to shelve.

- A hypothesis is a story that predicts user behavior when a variable (i.e. a change) is introduced. A hypothesis should include only one variable.

- The elements of a hypothesis include the area or functionality being studied, the variable, the metric being tracked, and the predicted outcome. Though it is not necessarily included in the hypothesis statement, it is important to state why you expect the variable to impact user behavior.

- Moving from a set of questions to a hypothesis is an intuitive leap. You'll want to think through what the observations and questions tell you about the audience. Create hypotheses that address audience and company goals.

- I listed a few tips that will help when building a hypothesis, including trying to prove yourself wrong, controlling your assumptions and keeping your audience in mind.

- You are likely to end up with more hypotheses than you have the resources or audience volume to test, so you will need to prioritize them. Factors to consider are confidence, impact, risk, cost, scope, timeline and dependencies.

Hypotheses

Susan builds on her deductions and questions from the previous step to form hypotheses.

In the previous section, Susan identified the B2C (consumer) group as the best group to focus on. Since they make most of the purchases, a small percentage improvement in sales will increase revenue more than a large improvement in the B2B (business) market.

Susan reviews her ideas and decides to create four

hypotheses. She'll focus on filtering for allergens, creating a new tool for building your own cake, improving the visibility of special occasion cakes, and increasing product image size.

Susan walks through the steps to create a hypothesis for allergens:

- Area:
  - Allow users to find baked goods without allergens

- Variable:
  - Revealing allergen information to users

- Why:
  - This is showing up as important in multiple places, i.e. in internal search and reports from customer support. In addition, the customers who care about allergens are likely to care about them very much.

- Metric:
  - Revenue

- Predicted Outcome:
  - Uncertain but estimated at 10% based on internal site search behavior

- Hypothesis:
  - When users can find allergen-free baked

goods revenue will increase by 10%.

Susan repeats this process and creates hypotheses for the rest of her ideas. She also considers what site changes are needed and how the hypotheses should be prioritized. Susan summarizes the information for her hypotheses:

Allergen Hypothesis

Hypothesis: When users can find allergen-free baked goods revenue will increase by 10%.

Site Change: All pages that list products include filters in the sidebar. Customers can filter by the size of the cake, price and flavor. Susan proposes that they add an allergen filter that would allow users to check one, all or none of: Gluten Free, No Nuts, No Eggs, Dairy Free, No Soy. (The Fancy Cake Company already collects this information so it would just be a matter of exposing it.) Susan works with the engineers and designer to get a scope estimate.

Prioritization Factors:

- Scope: Medium
- Timeline: Medium
- Confidence: High
- Impact: 10%
- Risk: Incorrectly labeled baked goods that contain allergens

- Cost: Low
- Dependencies: None

A possible risk associated with the allergen hypothesis is that baked goods labeled as allergen-free contain allergens. Susan circulates her concerns within the company. The legal team and the executives are not concerned about moving forward with this change, though, as they are confident the baked goods are labeled correctly.

"Build Your Own Cake" Hypothesis

Hypothesis: Adding a "Build Your Own Cake" tool would increase site revenue. However, the exact revenue increase is difficult to estimate.

Site Change: Susan doesn't go into great depth with this hypothesis but sketches out a rough idea of how it could work. She shares the idea with the engineering and design teams. As a result, the estimate for the scope is uncertain but should be directionally correct.

Prioritization Factors:

- Scope: Very Large
- Timeline: Long
- Confidence: Low
- Impact: Unknown
- Risk: High investment with low customer use

- Cost: A contractor would be required to build and maintain the tool
- Dependencies: None

Special Occasions Hypothesis

Hypothesis: Making it easy for the audience to find special occasion cakes will increase revenue by 5%.

Site Change: Susan proposes adding a new section to the site navigation. She works with the engineering and design teams to get a feel for the project size. They will need to rely on titles (e.g. a cake called Birthday Cake) and information submitted by the artisan bakeries. (This information is collected and checked each time a new product is added to the site so it is reliable.)

Prioritization Factors:

- Scope: Small
- Timeline: Short
- Confidence: Low
- Impact: 5%
- Risk: Very low
- Cost: Low
- Dependencies: None

Large Image Hypothesis

Hypothesis: Including large, attractive images of the cakes and other baked goods will increase revenue by 10%.

Site Change: Susan works with a designer to develop ideas for how to display larger images on the product pages. She also works with the engineers to understand how difficult the changes are.

Prioritization Factors:

- Scope: Large
- Timeline: Medium to Long
- Confidence: Medium
- Impact: 10%
- Risk: Very low
- Cost: Low
- Dependencies: None

Prioritization

Susan reviews her hypotheses and thinks about which ones she wants to focus on. She moves forward with the Allergen, Special Occasion and Large Image Hypotheses as they have a minimal downside and a potentially high upside.

The Build Your Own Cake Hypothesis appeals strongly

to Susan. The risk level, though, is high. It has significant resource and monetary costs associated with it and it is uncertain whether customers will respond well to it. Susan decides not to pursue this hypothesis.

Based on her personal opinion and the Fancy Cake Company's political environment, her tentative prioritization is:

- Allergen
- Special Occasions
- Large Image

She prioritizes the Allergen Hypothesis first as she has high confidence it will work (there's enough data supporting the decision) and the scope and timeline are reasonable. She places Special Occasions second – there's not much data supporting it, but it looks like an easy project and could be a nice win. Finally she places Large Image third as it's a harder change, even though it has a relatively high predicted impact.

(In a different situation, Susan might have prioritized these hypotheses differently. For instance, in an aggressive, ideas-driven company where she had already proven her ability, she might have included the Build Your Own Cake hypothesis in the top three. It is potentially a good way to expand market share.)

Step 5: Testing

In the first step, you developed a site objective with a clearly defined goal. By focusing on a specific goal, you can be smarter about what projects you take on and it is easier to make significant progress.

You gathered observations from multiple sources to learn about the audience, the site, and the business. Based on these observations, you developed a set of questions. You refined and improved these questions and created hypotheses, then decided which ones to test.

As you moved from observations to hypotheses, you've drawn a tighter and tighter focus on what to change, using the site objective as your guiding principle.

This chapter covers testing hypotheses and finding out if your ideas are right or if they need refinement.

Testing the audience

When you run tests, you are not testing the site. You are testing the audience and how the audience reacts to the change. Without the audience, the site is just a collection of code. A site cannot react or change its behavior; the audience of the site can. This distinction is easy to lose track of, but important to remember when setting up audience-facing tests and interpreting results.

Since it is the audience that you're testing, if the make up of the audience changes, the test results become suspect.

This is not an altogether comforting thought because the success of your site is determined by an ever-shifting population. The good news is that unless there is a major disruption or your product radically changes, your audience probably won't change too much too quickly. And testing will help you keep up with these gradual shifts.

You usually see two types of results when testing: the general and the audience specific.

You can apply general results over different sites with a reasonable expectation of success. They're changes like making the call to action button clearly visible, making the content easier to follow, or developing the most effective way to phrase copy. These can be lumped loosely together as best practices.

Audience-specific results are hard to predict as they depend on the unique characteristics of your audience. For example, your audience might respond better to extremely long, detailed text than to short, benefits-focused text. A product can also cause an audience to react unusually. Suppose you're promoting a product which is not like any product seen before; it's a brand-new technology and solution. You need to work harder to explain the product and communicate the benefits. So you might include more information on your product pages than would be best practice for a well-established technology.

The reason you can't skip testing and just rely on best practices is that best practices don't always hold true, or only hold partially true. Audiences vary. What works for one audience group may not work for others.

How to test

I've run through a few ways to test below. They have their strengths and weaknesses and are suitable for different stages of testing a hypothesis.

Thought experiments

Thought experiments are typically quick and work well for hypothesis testing in the early stages of refining, or rejecting, a hypothesis.

How it works

Look for data to validate or invalidate the hypothesis. Constant curiosity and a desire to dig deeply into what's going on is necessary for this approach to work.

The questions to ask are:

- What would you expect to find in the data to support your idea?
- What would you not expect to find in the data?
- What could you find in the data that would disprove your idea?

Let's walk through an example together.

The marketing department released a new campaign. The campaign targeted Millennials who graduated from a 4-year college within the past 8 years and had an income of at least $60K a year. It launched at the beginning of June. There was a slight increase in traffic from people clicking on the ads. Independent of this, though, the site traffic exploded. Visits to the site were up by 20% starting one week after the ad campaign launched. But revenue did not increase.

The marketing department is very excited about this as it looks like they have a new vertical with high levels of disposable income.

Based on these results, there's an opportunity to improve site conversion. You consider how to change the site to better capture this audience segment.

At this point you have an early hypothesis that says: Revise the site to better capture the Millennial market and so increase revenue. (Obviously this is still rough, but it's fine for a hypothesis before it's revised into its final form.)

You're puzzled, though, why there is a 20% increase in traffic but there's been no increase in revenue. The working idea is the site doesn't convert this audience well, which is why changing the site makes sense. But this doesn't sound right to you so you decide to dig into the data more.

What you find is that direct traffic accounts for only 10% of this increase and referral traffic accounts for the remaining 90%. It looks like a referral spam attack started right around when the marketing campaign went out, so the referral traffic increase is junk. The increase in non-spam traffic was about 2%, which is well within the normal variations in traffic numbers.

Since the traffic increase was so low, it reduces the justification for reworking the site to better target Millennials and the project is shelved. You used data to disprove your hypothesis. (And also incidentally the marketing department's results, but that's a whole other story.)

This example showed rejecting a hypothesis because it was based on bad data. Generally the revisions during thought experiments aren't so dramatic. Usually thought experiments lead to revising a slightly incorrect hypothesis into something stronger and more compelling.

Advantages and disadvantages

The advantage of thought experiments is that they take up very few resources and they're quick. You can discover interesting information about your audience and its behavior that you might have missed otherwise.

When you run thought experiments you refine your hypotheses, or throw them out, without using up too many resources. Because you refine the hypotheses, the tests you put live on the site are more likely to work.

The obvious disadvantage to thought experiments is that nothing changes on the site. While you can support or revise a hypothesis, it won't result in any customer facing changes. You won't see any improvement in your metrics.

Since the thought experiments are not customer facing, another limitation is that you can only check your hypothesis with the information you already have. If some of that information is bad or misleading, you can draw incorrect conclusions.

It's not precisely a disadvantage, but a problem you will sometimes face is incidental damage to other people's stories. You might turn up information that undercuts reported results. How to handle that depends on the internal politics of the company. However, it is much better to know before you make site changes that the data is bad than to be blamed when the site changes don't work.

When to use

Thought experiments are incredibly useful for a first-round check of a hypothesis. You can use thought experiments to detect errors and refine your hypothesis before you make site changes.

Usability testing

Usability testing can be done at any stage, including on a live site. In this section, I'll discuss usability testing before the designs go live, e.g. at the wireframe stage.

The advantage of running usability testing early on is to make sure you've not introduced usability issues. You can also run an initial test of a usability-driven hypothesis.

How it works

If you base your design change on a correct hypothesis but the design change introduces usability issues, then your hypothesis can fail even though the idea is correct. This gives you a false negative when you test your hypothesis. So long as bad usability isn't inherent to the hypothesis, if you run a usability test you can identify and correct the issue before you launch.

To put an example around this, Edmund hypothesizes that his audience needs additional technical specifications before making a purchase. However, adding the technical specifications pushes the buy button down the page.

When Edmund runs usability testing, he finds that users have difficulty figuring out how to buy the product. Because of the results of the usability testing, Edmund changes the design so the buy button is more visible.

The test version with the additional technical specifications outperformed the control. If Edmund had not improved the buy button's visibility, the test would have failed. Not because adding technical specifications was the wrong idea, but because of a usability flaw.

There are many ways to perform usability testing, and even the less sophisticated approaches can provide useful insights. Approaches include using online software, setting up a small test on people who fit your target audience, or employing an outside agency.

Advantages and disadvantages

The big advantage of usability testing before you launch changes is that it helps you to spot poor design features that trip up your audience. This can save you all sorts of headaches and expenses, and prevent your hypotheses from failing because of a usability issue.

A disadvantage is that it is hard to re-create your users' frame of mind when performing usability testing. For instance, if you're usability testing a purchase flow, then reassuring copy about returns is not too critical because the testers aren't actually buying the product. It can make a huge difference on a live site, though, if customers are worried about what will happen if they don't like the product. Usability testing will find areas where people have a problem with completing a task, but it isn't as effective at finding areas where the site is not addressing the users' emotional state.

The small size of the testing group can distort your results.
It's difficult to find a set of people who perfectly reflect your audience segments and behave like the average member of an

audience segment. This is not a reason to skip usability testing, but it is a reason to interpret your results carefully.

When to use

When you are making changes to test a hypothesis, running usability tests can help you catch usability issues before the test goes live. Run usability testing early on when it is still easy to change course.

Site testing

In site testing's simplest form, you test your original version against a new version to see which one performs better. If the new one wins, it proves your hypothesis; if it loses, your hypothesis fails.

How it works

In a simple A/B test, you run both the original and the test versions at the same time. The person setting up the test defines what percentage of the audience will be part of the test. However, the software randomly determines whether a visitor goes into the control or test group. All versions are run concurrently which helps to minimize environmental variables such as marketing campaigns and changes in the competitive landscape.

In practice, this means that if the test version outcompetes the control it is probably because of differences introduced with the test version.

Let's set up a simple A/B test as an example. Suppose you wanted to test a banner promotion on the homepage. The original version reads "50% off cashmere tops". The new test version reads "Buy 1 cashmere top, get 1 free."

You set the audience to be split evenly between the two versions. The metric is revenue generated by sales of cashmere tops.

You run the test and get interesting results. The test version clearly outperforms the original with a 10% increase in sales. Your audience responds more strongly to the 'buy 1 get 1 free' approach.

During this time, though, the revenue for cashmere tops dropped by 15% overall. This is odd. You research the drop and discover that changes in the social landscape caused people to be less enthusiastic about cashmere.

Here's why this is important. If you had just switched to the new promotion without testing against the old, it would have looked like there was a drop in sales, even though the new promotion outperformed the old one. Because you A/B tested, you could tell the test version improved results even though overall revenue dropped.

As well as simple A/B/N testing, another common approach is to use multivariate testing. Generally a multivariate site test includes multiple changes run at the same time in different combinations. All combinations are tested. (Some multivariate testing methods use a subset of possible combinations. However, site testing systems typically run every version.)

For instance, on one page you might test two different button colors and two different hero images. In a multivariate experiment, you would run the following five combinations:

- Control, i.e. the original unchanged version
- 1st button + 1st hero image
- 2nd button + 2nd hero image
- 1st button + 2nd hero image
- 2nd button + 1st hero image

Multivariate tests require a high audience volume because so many versions are being tested. However, it is an easy way to test multiple changes in one experiment and to find interactions between the elements you're testing.

Advantages and disadvantages

There are several advantages to site testing.

The critical advantage is the obvious one. As far as you can, you're controlling for environmental factors by running the test version and the original at the same time. If the test is set up and run correctly, then any change you see is because of the variable.

Site testing also saves a lot of internal arguing. You can run a test rather than having extremely long discussions about whether, for instance, an orange or green button will be more effective.

A well set up and correctly run test gives you results that you can build on. Whether it succeeds or fails, the results give you a good idea of what's going on with your audience.

If you're making major site changes, you can test them out on a subset of your population rather than releasing them universally. It is hard to roll back a universal change that your audience responds poorly to, but comparatively easy to roll back a test version.

There are also some disadvantages, though.

Test results are not permanently correct. The fundamental reason is that audiences shift. The audience who shows up on your site in June may be different than the audience in December. So the site change that showed a huge lift in June may not apply in December. A fundamental weakness of testing is that the audience changes over time and so old test results may no longer be valid.

Because of this weakness, companies should rerun tests at later times to make sure they remain valid. This doesn't always happen for several reasons. No one wants to go back and say that the site change that was a winner is no longer working. It's hard to get executives invested in this type of testing – they would typically rather keep moving forward than test something that's already been tested. And it's just not as interesting as running a new test.

Another potential weakness is stacking the deck, either intentionally or unintentionally. Stacking the deck will give you unrealistic results. To take a simplistic example, suppose your goal is to increase the number of clicks on a button. The most effective way to do so might be to remove all content from the page except the button. Users would click on it just to get to the next page. But the change is not adding value to the user experience and the winning test isn't telling you anything. Knowing how you expect your audience to react to a variable and why helps to prevent you from stacking the deck accidentally because you'll think about the user experience.

On sites with low audience volume, tests can take a very long time or it can even be impossible to determine a winner. If there aren't enough people coming to your site, you can't get a statistically significant result in a realistic time frame.

Finally, some testing systems can only test single pages. For example, if you want to change the color of the text on every product page, some systems can't do that. However, the exact restrictions vary significantly by testing system.

Concerns about site testing

There are concerns about the accuracy of the results calculated by testing platforms. At least one company has changed how it runs calculations because of these concerns. I strongly recommend you research how results are calculated before choosing a testing system. Make sure you are comfortable with the trade offs and how the software declares a winning or losing test.

When to use

Site testing is a good choice when you have the necessary volume to get statistically significant results and the technical resources to implement the tests. It is also a great way to find out if a site change will be successful before rolling it out to your entire audience.

Site testing is helpful in very political or confrontational environments as you can show whether a change is working or not without it becoming a matter of opinion.

Tracking data

This approach is prone to error, but it is sometimes the *only* option available for tracking the impact of audience-facing changes. Typically this is useful on sites that have significant technical hurdles or resource issues that prevent site testing.

If your company has an analyst, this is a good project to involve them in. They have tools and procedures that will help you determine if the site changes are working. Since the analyst will be less emotionally invested in the outcome of the site changes, the analysis is more likely to be correct.

How it works

Monitor a site change's impact by tracking your key metric (e.g. revenue) directly before and after a site change. Use as long a period of time as possible before and after the change.

The longer a period of time you take, the more useful the

information you gather is likely to be. For instance, if you look at only a week on either side of the change, normal shifts in user behavior could obscure your results.

However, if you look at too long a period, then changes in the site environment can make the comparison inaccurate, e.g. marketing campaigns and competitive landscape changes.

One way to control for problems in your data is to keep close track of any variables that could affect the results. For this to work, you must keep excellent records and have a reliable analytics system.

I've listed a few common variables, but this only scratches the surface. There will be other variables specific to your industry, company and situation.

- Seasonality: Look at what happened in previous years and account for seasonality. For instance, if you launch a change in May and revenue typically goes down in June, you'll need to account for that drop when you make the before and after comparison.

- Holidays: On a similar note, for most businesses, revenue goes down during holidays. If a holiday before or after the change depressed revenue, account for that in your calculations.

- Day of the Week: Account for differences in day-of-the-week behavior. Suppose your revenue is almost nonexistent over the weekends, but strong on weekdays. Make sure the comparison periods have the same number of weekends or account for the difference in some other way.

- Outliers: Know what your typical order pattern looks like. For instance, if you average order value is $60 but four times a year you get a $6,000 purchase, that may be enough to upset your calculations. You'd need to pull out the outlier purchases.

- Site Errors: Keep track of site errors that could impact the metric you're tracking. For instance, if your site went down for two hours in the middle of a busy day, that can impact the revenue totals.

When running this type of analysis, be wary of confirmation bias. Confirmation bias is a tendency to accept information we agree with and ignore or discount information we don't agree with. It is a huge problem in this type of analysis. Be skeptical of how you analyze the data. Make sure you have a good reason for anything you adjust, especially if it is in favor of your hypothesis.

Results

If possible, have an analyst review your conclusions or run the analysis. The analyst will be less prone to confirmation bias and probably has a background in statistics.

Your results will be directional rather than precise. If the change you made is significant enough, though, you should be able to see its impact.

Advantages and disadvantages

Assuming everything is controlled for properly, and the change is big enough, you can get a feel for whether the change worked or not.

An indirect advantage is that this type of analysis is an excellent way to learn a lot about what is happening on the site. It requires such an in-depth knowledge of factors that impact your results that you gain significant insight into the site and audience behavior.

The major disadvantage is that comparing data before and after a change is imprecise. You won't get exact numbers and if you haven't accounted for all the factors that could impact your numbers, your analysis may be wrong.

When to use

The time to use this approach is when you want to test audience-facing changes but there are significant hurdles that prevent you from using a testing system.

Combined approach

I've covered thought experiments, usability testing, site testing and tracking data as separate approaches. In practice they can all work together.

Use thought experiments to test and refine hypotheses before you make any changes to the site. Run usability tests to make sure you haven't unintentionally added a usability issue before you push changes live. Employ site testing to get a good idea of what lift the site changes produce. Track data to understand how the site is behaving and to confirm that the site changes improve results in the long term.

Analyzing test results

When running an audience-facing test, there are three groups of results:

- *It worked!* This is great. You drew the correct conclusions and you can move forward with a new and improved site. This is the best result.

- *The change made your site worse.* The test version under-performed by a significant margin. This is not good, but at least you can learn something from it. Think about why the test failed. Asking why a test failed is useful because it gives you new insight into your audience.

- *There was no change.* These are my least favorite results because it's hard to know what to do with them. Was the site change something the audience doesn't care about? Is the site change important but no better than the control? Is there something else in the user flow that's stopping users from reaching the goal you're testing for, so the results look flat? This type of result is frustrating and hard to interpret.

No matter what the results are, always try to answer why you saw the results you did. If you just make a note of the impact on your metric without thinking about your audience, you'll miss a lot of the value of testing. Tests are a wonderful tool for checking your assumptions and learning about your audience. The more you understand about your audience, the more effective a site you can build and the smarter you can be about future changes.

Documentation

This is hard to believe when you first start testing, but it is incredibly easy to lose track of details of previous tests. This is especially true if you're making incremental changes.

It is important to keep the details straight, though. You may need to refer back to a test because subsequent data has changed how you interpret results. You may need to pull together a presentation that details how the site has changed. And you'll add the test results to your observations so you'll want them to be as accurate and complete as possible.

What to document

It is a good idea to document any user-facing tests. This includes usability testing, site testing and tracking data. On occasion, you may want to document thought experiments.

Don't rely on a testing system to document. Typically testing systems do a rotten job at preserving information other than the test results. For example, while the testing system may record that you tested the homepage, it won't record what the homepage looked like.

Below I've listed some of the information you'll want to document, but build on this list as needed.

Dates

When was the test started? When did it end?

This is useful for a few reasons. For instance, after the test, you might discover there was a change in the competitive landscape. You can compare the dates of the disruption to the time you ran the test. If there's an overlap, it may alter your interpretation of the results.

Hypothesis

When you constructed the hypothesis, you also thought about why the hypothesis would succeed. Include both the hypothesis and the *why* in your documentation.

Visual record

For almost all tests, recording the appearance of what you are testing is helpful. For A/B and multivariate tests that would be the control and test versions. For usability testing, it might be the wireframes shown to users. For tracking data, it would be the before and after versions of the page.

An image is invaluable for jogging the memory. A visual record of the losing versions can also help remind you what to avoid.

As well as the visual documentation, describe each version. The details of the test will be more obvious with a written description.

Results

In the results section, record which versions won or lost and by how much. If you can, also include the statistical significance of the results. While the testing system will record the results, it's helpful to include them with your other documentation.

Include your interpretation of the outcome in this section. What did the results mean? Did they tell you anything you didn't know or didn't expect? Did it confirm an idea you already held?

Next test

Do the test results suggest any follow up tests you should run in the future? If so, make sure to record the ideas for future tests.

Actions taken

Because of this test, what, if anything, did you change on the site? For instance, if you ran an A/B test, did one of the test versions replace the original control? If you didn't make any change to the site because of the test results, include that in the notes as well.

You may also want to note why the test ended. This isn't always necessary but it can be helpful when you're reviewing the testing history.

Chapter summary

- When you test hypotheses, you find out if they're correct, in need of refinement, or incorrect.
- Add the results from the tests to your observations. They'll influence later questions and hypotheses.
- When you run tests on your site, you're not actually testing the site – what you're testing is the audience's reaction to the site. If the audience changes over time then testing results may no longer be valid.
- There are two broad categories of test results: General results that can be applied over many sites and audience-specific results that are hard to predict and often only apply to a specific audience.
- We looked at four testing approaches: thought experiments, usability testing, site testing and tracking data.

They are useful under different circumstances and all have their advantages and disadvantages.

- When performing thought experiments, look for data that proves or disproves your hypothesis. While you may uncover data that had previously been overlooked, thought experiments are not an audience-facing test. They are useful for refining hypotheses.

- Usability testing is useful as an early reality check on how users interact with the design changes. It is also a way to avoid false negatives created by poor usability when testing your hypothesis.

- When you run a site test, you present different versions to your audience and measure how they react. The great advantage of this approach is it helps to control for variables that impact your whole audience. For instance, if a new competitor moves into your space and drives down overall revenue it will impact each version you're testing equally.

- Tracking data is a difficult testing approach to do well. With this method, you track and compare audience behavior before and after a change. If the change is significant enough, you can usually see a change in the audience behavior. But you can't be sure whether another unidentified factor is impacting your results.

- The strongest approach is to make use of all four testing strategies. Refine hypotheses with thought experiments, check for pre-launch issues with usability testing, run site tests, and make sure the improvements hold true by tracking data.

- Whether you have a winning or losing test, consider what the test results tell you about your audience's state of mind and motivations.

- Make sure you document all test results. As well as other notes, documentation should include the hypothesis, results, and what action was taken as a result of the test.

Testing

Susan, who works at the Fancy Cake Company, has developed several hypotheses. Her goal is to increase revenue from the Fancy Cake Company website.

Susan reviews her hypotheses and starts thinking about how she should test each one.

Allergen

Susan plans to add extra filters to the sidebar so users can choose baked goods that don't have allergens. Susan starts by running a usability test on the changes. The new design tests well and no significant issues are found.

After researching the site testing system and talking to the engineers, Susan discovers that there is no way to

A/B test the Allergen Hypothesis. As a result she'll have to track data to see how the pages perform once the extra filters are added.

The site changes are made to FancyCakeCompany.com. Susan works with an analyst. Together they identify environmental variables that could distort the results. The analyst runs the numbers and reports a 7% improvement in results.

Susan goes one step further. She looks at how many of the cakes now sorted under allergens sold before and after the change. She also looks at visits to the allergen-filtered pages. Susan sees a large increase in the number of cakes sold that are allergen sensitive. She also sees a significant number of visits that filtered for allergens. This information suggests that while adding an allergen filter resulted in a relatively modest increase in overall revenue, it is an important addition to a subset of users.

Susan adds this information to her observations and shares it with the team that manages the artisan bakery relationships. They communicate it to the bakeries and more allergen-free baked goods are submitted to the site. The allergen-free baked goods generate more and more revenue over time.

Special Occasions

Susan proposes adding a new section to the site that groups baked goods by occasion. Her confidence is low for this hypothesis because she doesn't have a lot of information. Susan decides she'll run thought experiments before any other testing because they're quick and cheap. If everything looks okay, this will be an easy change to A/B test.

Susan reviews her observations. She created this hypothesis because Customer Service reported that people regularly call in about cakes for special occasions.

Susan thinks about other ways she could find out about audience interest in special occasion cakes. She reviews the results from user interviews but discovers they've not addressed this particular question.

Susan also looks at how the bakeries tag their products and notices that many of them include tags such as birthday cake and Christmas cake. This doesn't tell her the audience's level of interest directly, but it does tell her that the bakeries think it's important information.

As a more direct measure of the audience's interest, Susan looks at the internal site search report. She sees a lot of searches for wedding cakes and birthday cakes, and to a lesser extent retirement, Christmas and Easter cakes. Combined, these make up about 15% of all searches.

Based on this information, Susan changes her confidence in the Special Occasion hypothesis from low to high. She also changes her predicted revenue increase from 5% to 10%.

Susan runs the A/B test on the site and it does much better than expected. The revenue increase is 15%.

Susan notices that as the test runs, the difference between the revenue per day from the test and the control increases. In other words, later in the experiment, people in the test group become more likely to buy.

Susan isn't sure why more purchases are being made in the test group later in the experiment. One possibility is that some people buy cakes immediately, but others come back later to buy cakes they bookmarked. As the special occasion filtering is new, some of the revenue could be delayed as people leave and then come back to purchase the special occasion cake. (This lines up with one of her earlier observations that direct traffic often lands on a product page.)

When Susan digs into the results further, she finds that birthday cakes make up a significant portion of the revenue increase. Most of the increase, though, is from wedding cakes. She adds this information to her observations. The results inspire a series of hypotheses about how to present wedding cakes on the site. The marketing team also builds several successful campaigns around wedding cakes.

Large Image

Susan plans to A/B test larger images on the product pages. She works with a designer to put together a comp, and then, because it is such a large change, runs usability testing with a small group. The participants have a hard time finding the "add to cart" button. The designer modifies the design and Susan runs a second round of usability testing. This time there are no issues.

The engineering team implements the new pages and the A/B test goes live. The results are disappointing. Revenue is 5% lower for pages with the larger images than for the original version.

Susan is puzzled so she spends some time comparing the control versus the test. She's reasonably confident there is not a usability issue. Susan suspects it may be one of two possibilities:

- Perhaps people are not that interested in how the baked goods look. This seems intuitively unlikely as many food sites, blogs and online recipes feature large images of food.
- To make room for the larger images and to keep a prominent placement for the buy button, the designer pushed the biographical information about the bakeries down the page. Perhaps the biographical information is important to the people who are purchasing the baked goods. They are

interested in the story behind the food as it makes them feel good.

Susan adds this information to the observations and it helps her form insights into audience motivations.

Results

Susan pulls together her results from the first round of testing:

- Allergen Hypothesis: 7% improvement in revenue
- Special Occasions Hypothesis: 15% improvement in revenue
- Large Image Hypothesis: 5% decrease in revenue

Susan rolls out the winning changes to the entire site. Based on her test results, she expects a greater than 20% improvement in overall revenue.

Susan's test results spur new insights:

- Special occasion cakes, especially wedding cakes, are profitable on the site and may also be profitable in other marketing initiatives such as newsletters.

- As a side effect of the new special occasions section, the B2B sales went up at the end of the year.

Although there was no direct testing to verify it, Susan believes the increase in B2B sales was because the site changes made it easier to find holiday cakes.

- Allergens are important to a subset of users. The number of allergen-labeled cakes sold on the site continued to increase after the testing period ended.

- The Large Image test netted negative results. However, the results suggest the story behind the baked goods is important. The larger images may or may not have been the problem. Susan can pursue these ideas in later experiments.

Step 6: The Big Picture

The final step of the scientific method is to create theories. Scientists use experimental evidence to form theories that explain phenomenon observed in the natural world. Theories are predictive. If new evidence contradicts the theory or shows it no longer predicts behavior correctly, the theory is modified or replaced.

For website changes, the evidence isn't strong enough to create a theory. However, you can create a big picture idea that connects what you have learned and that explains and predicts user behavior.

The big picture

In the Six Steps, you expand your knowledge by conducting research and running tests. You follow the evidence to new insights.

Following the evidence will take you in directions you won't expect – you'll make discoveries that aren't obvious. And as you go through the steps, you'll learn more about your audience, especially from unexpected discoveries.

The big picture is a story about your audience drawn from the evidence you have gathered. It helps to explain *why* users behave the way they do. By developing a big picture that ties evidence together, you can more accurately predict how your audience will react to site changes.

One way to approach constructing the big picture is to divide your evidence into groups and then look for patterns and overlaps. The inner group is information that you have high confidence in. One step out is information which is probably true, but is not certain. On the outer ring is speculation or poorly supported information. Develop insights from patterns in behavior, unexpected correlations, and discrepancies. Use these insights to create a larger view of what's going on with the audience.

I realize this is a little soft around the edges, but inferring human motivations from data *is* a little soft around the edges. It's a matter of taking the output and working backward to what it means about the person who acted.

Why it matters

The more information you have, the richer the picture and the better you understand your audience. The big picture explains why site changes worked in the past and helps you predict how your audience will react in the future. With a big picture, what would have seemed like a wild idea before you gathered all the information becomes an obvious and conservative one.

You could follow steps one through five, and you'd get great results, but you'd be missing a significant pay off. You would not see how your results and observations tie together. With a big picture you can develop a strategy for how the site should work rather than reacting to problems with individual parts of the site. This insight is valuable when you decide what to change on your current site and how to build the next iteration.

The best outcomes

The Six Steps is an on-going process. As you improve the site, you will add to your observations, questions, hypotheses and test results. Your big picture view of the audience will become richer and more nuanced. As you know more, you can make better decisions to improve your audience's response. The more you know, the better your ideas. And when you act on your best ideas, you get the best outcomes.

Chapter summary

- Scientists construct theories based on evidence. A theory explains and predicts phenomena. The level of certainty required to create theories is not realistic on a website, but you can develop a big picture that explains and predicts audience behavior.

- The big picture pulls together evidence to create a larger story about how the audience behaves and why. If you can understand the why, you can better predict what changes your audience will respond well to in the future.

The big picture

Over the past 12 months, Susan had the goal of increasing revenue from the website by 50%.

She met and exceeded the 50% improvement goal. Through her work she learned a lot about the Fancy Cake Company's audiences.

With the information covered earlier in this book and the results of other tests and research, Susan develops a big picture understanding of what motivates the audience groups and how she can reach them better.

Susan expects that how well she understands her audience will improve as she learns more, but she has divided the audience into three types of users based on the information she has now:

- Everyday consumers
- Businesses
- Wedding cake purchasers

Everyday consumers

The everyday consumers have the lowest average order

value. However, they make repeat purchases and are the largest group. They make up the backbone of the site revenue. Their purchases are typically for birthdays, social gatherings or home consumption.

They respond well to information about the bakeries they are buying from. A sense of personal connection with the bakeries is important to them. The status element of purchasing high-cost baked goods impacts their decisions. They perceive themselves as being nonconformist because they don't buy from corporations. However, they conform within their social group by making purchases from artisans. The baked goods' appearance is important, but not the only consideration.

Susan's plans for this group: Susan notices that a good chunk of this group buys baked goods regularly. She plans to launch a Baker of the Month program which will deliver a selection of baked goods from a different artisan bakery each month. Susan wants to see if she can entice these buyers to be more frequent customers. She'll appeal to their interest in the backstories and the excitement of an unpredictable collection of baked goods delivered every month. Since there is a strong status component, she will make it easy to give the Baker of the Month subscription as a gift.

Businesses

Business purchases are also important, but their purchasing is mostly during the holidays. There are relatively few businesses that buy cakes from the Fancy Cake Company. However, the businesses make large purchases and send out cakes to many people. The appeal of the Fancy Cake Company is that it is an easy way for companies to send out high-quality local cakes. The purchasing process is streamlined so it doesn't take up too many resources or too much time. Because these are business gifts, appearance is important. The backstories of the bakeries, beyond the fact that they're local, aren't too critical.

Susan's plans for this group: Susan thinks that the Fancy Cake Company has not reached out to businesses enough. She plans to work with marketing and sales to find new ways to reach businesses and discover how the site can help support these efforts. For example, adding custom landing pages and discounts for large orders to the site.

Wedding

Wedding cakes are a newer addition to the site so Susan has less data about the wedding audience group. As with the business group, there is some seasonality. Most customers purchase wedding cakes during the summer months. This group has the potential to be extremely valuable. Wedding cakes are deeply important to the people who buy them. The most passionate bakery reviews are the ones tied to wedding cakes. These reviews have a stronger impact on future sales than those for any other audience group. This audience group is strongly motivated by appearance and by the status implied by the cake. They are also highly emotionally invested in the cakes. The customers view them as a part of the larger story of their wedding day rather than as a cake.

Susan's plans for this group: Susan plans to create an online tool where couples can work with artisan bakeries to create their perfect wedding cake. These cakes will be completely customizable and sold for a premium. If successful, this will significantly increase the site's average order value and overall revenue.

Conclusion

I've covered a lot in this book, so in this section, I'll go over some key takeaways. I'll review each step, discuss the advantages of the Six Steps as well as other uses for this approach, and finish with next steps.

Six Steps

The scientific method is the essential tool that scientists use to make discoveries. Advances in medicine, biology, chemistry, physics and other branches of science were made by employing this method. It is a building block of the modern world.

The Six Steps are based on the scientific method, adjusted for the realities of website work. The Six Steps move from identifying the problem through to forming a big picture idea of the audience. By following the Six Steps you gain insights into your audience, find new opportunities, and predict what your audience will respond well to.

Step 1: Define the problem

Build a site objective by researching company goals and challenges, and talking to stakeholders. The site objective includes your goal and what problem you need to solve.

A site objective helps you to stay focused. With this focus you can achieve better results more quickly because you'll be able to sort out what's important from what's a distraction.

Step 2: Observations

In step two, gather information about your audience, the company and how the company is positioned.

This information can come from multiple places, including internal sources, your own analysis and industry thought leaders. It's surprising how much information is available once you start looking. Usually the biggest challenge isn't a lack of information but deciding how reliable the information is.

Observations are the basis for evidence-based decisions, which have lower bias and are more accurate than decisions made exclusively on hunches or emotion. In the longer term, evidence-based decisions have a higher success rate.

Step 3: Questions

This is a fun step – this is where you pull together the

observations, turn them into deductions, and form questions.

In this book, I covered how to create a table to organize observations, deductions and questions. This is a powerful technique to organize your thinking and find connections that might otherwise be hidden.

When you create questions you find areas of opportunity and begin to understand which ideas make the most sense to pursue.

Step 4: Hypotheses

Now that you have created the questions, you can narrow down to the most promising ideas and create testable hypotheses.

Hypotheses describe what you want to test and predict how it will impact user behavior. A hypothesis consists of multiple parts, including the variable and the metric you'll track.

Step 5: Testing

This is an exciting part of the process because you find out if you're right. In this step, you test hypotheses and find out if the site change will help you meet your goal. The test results also help you to get to know your audience better.

There are a few different ways to test: thought experiments, usability testing, site testing and data tracking. They all have their pros and cons and work best in combination with each other.

Step 6: The big picture

In this step, you pull together evidence to create a big picture. The big picture describes audience behavior and motivations.

The advantage of having a big picture is that you can use it to predict your audiences' behavior. This is helpful when improving the current site and critical when launching a new site.

Advantages

In the short term, using the Six Steps gets you away from biases and opinions and into reality-based decisions. Because your decisions are based on facts, they are more likely to be right and therefore successful.

In the longer term, your approach to the site improves. This is not a one-shot deal – you are constantly building on what you have learned. As you learn more, your information pool becomes richer. You can make smarter decisions, find areas of opportunity, and move much faster.

Finally, because you are making evidence-based decisions it becomes much easier to persuade other people to buy in to your proposals. As you rack up the successes you will find support for your projects easier to get, and you'll be able to take more calculated risks, leading to greater successes.

Uses

When you follow the Six Steps, you learn about your audience. The more you know about what your audience wants, why they want it, and how that lines up with your company's goals, the more effective your site will be.

The ideal is to help your audience achieve their goals and put them center stage in your decisions. After all, without an audience, your website is just taking up space on a server.

I am passionate about websites and I love improving them, so when I sat down to write a book, I wrote it about websites. But the Six Steps can be applied to more than just websites. Because it is audience focused, this approach works well when you need to understand what people do and do not respond to. The key requirements are that you have a large enough group to test and accurate data tracking.

While I focused in on optimizing websites, this process can be used across many different situations to gain clarity and accuracy, and drive great results.

What next?

The Six Steps require analytical and creative thought. While most people are capable of doing both, it's a common belief that an individual is only good at one or the other. This has the unfortunate effect of people choosing to focus on one and giving up on the other.

If you are creative, chances are you already use analytical approaches. For instance, you probably look at others' creative outputs, decide which ones are interesting, and their ideas influence your work. In other words, you collect observations, form conclusions about your observations, and apply those conclusions.

If you are analytical, you likely spend a fair amount of your time solving problems to increase the accuracy of your analysis. In other words, you bring in ideas from different places, create many possible solutions, and then choose the best one.

Don't decide that you are creative or analytical, but rather that you have a goal and you are going to win.

Having said all that, some mental muscles improve with practice.

If you have trouble thinking through problems...

Tools

There are many books that discuss mental tools for solving problems. A quick look online or in your local bookstore will turn up some options.

Practice

Look for problems to solve. For instance, site data is often a great place to look for problems. Search for areas where the site data is incomplete or inconsistent. Also, when you implement changes to your site analytics system, e.g. adding filters to your Google Analytics profile, don't just do them, think about unexpected impacts they might have. Think about other ways you can slice the data.

If you have trouble imagining your audience's motivations...

Read novels

Reading novels exposes you to other peoples' ideas. You get to see the world from the author's point of view with great depth and clarity. New readers often enjoy science fiction or fantasy, but if this doesn't appeal there are many options out there.

Make up stories

This is one of the more unusual suggestions, but it works. For instance, if the pen on your desk could think, what would it want? Why? Perhaps it would like to write a biography of the great pens in American history. It could start with Thomas Jefferson's quill, move on to the pens of the early astronauts, and end with the latest presidential signature. Why is it important to the pen to write this biography? What's stopping it? This is obviously nonsense as it's a pen, but this type of silly exercise is good practice for thinking about motivations.

If you have trouble creating questions...

Pick up a creative hobby

A new hobby can flex creative muscles and encourage you to think about the world in different ways. Developing a creative hobby will teach you to be more flexible and you'll have an easier time coming up with ideas.

Scribble down ideas

Think about the problem you want to solve. Then go away and do something else. When you come back, pull out paper and write down every possible solution that comes to mind. Don't judge your ideas, just write them down. Some of your ideas will be great. The trick is to be non-judgmental and to write down all your ideas even if they seem odd.

If you want to know more...

Read

You don't have to do it all by yourself. Make a habit of reading. Rely on the insights and observations of others to develop a better understanding of the world and the people who inhabit it.

Finally...

If these suggestions don't appeal to you, take a look around. There are many options, some of which will be perfect for you.

Acknowledgements

Thanks to my family for their support and encouragement. Without them this book would never have been more than an idea.

Special thanks to Kerry Granshaw for useful advice, to Tim Granshaw for his insights, and to Walt Grayson for his support.

Made in the USA
Monee, IL
04 November 2026

67377608R00095